PLAYdate

A parent's and teacher's guide to putting on a play

CINDY MARCUS

MERIWETHER PUBLISHING LTD.
Colorado Springs, Colorado

Meriwether Publishing Ltd., Publisher
PO Box 7710
Colorado Springs, CO 80933-7710

www.meriwether.com

Editor: Arthur L. Zapel
Cover and book design: Jan Melvin
Photographs: Annie Horak

Library of Congress Cataloging-in-Publication Data

Marcus, Cindy
    PLAYdate for kids : a parent's and teacher's guide to putting on a play / by Cindy Marcus. -- 1st ed.
        p. cm.
    ISBN 978-1-56608-160-3 (pbk.)
    1. Theater--Production and direction. 2. Playwriting. 3. Children's theater. I. Title. II. Title: Play date for kids.
    PN2053.M358 2009
    792.02'32--dc22
                                            2008041613

        1   2   3   09   10   11

For Finn and Flip

Table of Contents

Foreword

OK, so this book totally rocks. Not only is it an easy breezy read, which may have you giggling aloud at Starbucks and getting the evil-eye from those laptop-working, latte-sipping folks around you, but it's useful. It's practical. It works, baby.

It's hands on, and isn't that what life is about?

When I was in school, I was in as many plays as I could be in. I mean, everything. When the kid playing Uncle Henry dropped out of *Wizard of Oz,* I put on the overalls and a mustache and went on-stage! I even started to write songs for the musicals we were doing. I did that because I figured if I wrote the songs I was singing, then I would be sure to like them. But I found I loved doing it so much I wrote songs for other people in the plays too. I was acting, writing, and composing. Pretty much everything I do in my career now. Wow, and it all started with a play.

Nowadays the average annual budget for a school's theatre arts program is just a little below the price of a gallon of gas. How's the next generation supposed to get started with a play? Where will all the kids of today learn to write, compose, and act? How will they break through shyness, learn to speak in public, and be part of something larger than themselves?

Happily, the answer is right in your hands. This book encourages teachers, moms and dads, aunts and uncles, grammas and grampas, and any enthusiastic chronologically grown-up person to step up and make theatre happen. It's not just a bunch of cool suggestions that leave you with a pat on the back and a knot in your stomach. It's a step-by-step process for the brave soul willing to put on a play with kids.

Yes, it's daunting, yes, it's overwhelming, but with this book it's also amazingly doable. There is nothing like standing backstage after the curtain call with the applause still ringing in your ears. The beaming pride on my mom's and dad's face is still burned into my memory. It made me believe there's nothing I can't do.

Every kid deserves that feeling. And with your determination and this book, they can get it.

— Julie Brown

Award-winning writer and performer for TV (*Just Say Julie* MTV series), film (*Earth Girls Are Easy*) and *Goddess in Progress,* a comedy album of novelty songs.

Acknowledgments and Thank Yous

A million thank yous go into this book:

Art and Meriwether Publishing for believing in me.

Amy, editor extrordinaire

My Pioneer Drama Service family. You give great advice.

Mr. Flores for opening up his classroom to me. Jenny Turner for keeping that door open with her whole heart and soul.

Rene W., you made the fight fun and the journey worthwhile.

Cliff W., you bring it out of the kids.

Tami Hill, Kristin S., Diane O., and the other moms who got going when the tough got ... going.

Mrs. G. whose hugs and appreciation were beyond classy, they made me believe again.

The parents of the Old Orchard Foundation. You're the unsung heroes, until now. Laaaa, la, la!

The kids in Miss Turner's class: Jose, Jose, Jessica, Kara, Natalie, Jessica, Garrett, Collin, Jared, KC, Amy, Paul, Jett, Nick, Michael, Ivan, Luis, Finn, Kristin and Shannon.

Annie — daughter of my heart.

Dennis da' man, my bro in all things.

Ann, Brad, Dommy, Kimberly, Scott, and the rest of my "family." You guys keep me going.

And most important, my men: Finn, you are the best thing that ever happened to me. Flip, truly, madly, deeply forever. You are the dream.

Introduction: Why This Book?

"Mommy, Mr. Flores wants to talk to you."

Rip. Slash. Toss. That was the devastating sound of the arts program in my eight-year-old son's classroom. Music, theatre, dance, and fine art were all being eliminated. He and his classmates were never going to know the thrill of standing before a live audience and singing "I'm a Happy Turkey," or the pride of molding a lumpy clay snowman. Yet, in the end, these small milestones were an important part of his development.

What the Smart Guys Say

According to Richard Riley, the Secretary of Education under President Bill Clinton, "We are failing them, because we are blocking their ability to learn."

And he wasn't the only one concerned, " ... our perceptive, sense-based capacities have as much — if not more — to do with learning as our intellectual or rational capacities."[1]

" ... since drama has become an important method of understanding others and our own lives, children need to learn to appreciate, interpret, and evaluate it."[2]

But wait, there's more ...

"Research demonstrates that dramatic play has a strong impact on children's cognitive and social development as well as provides children with opportunities to learn to express their feelings and become sensitive to the values of others."[2]

James Catterall, the lead author of the study and an education professor at UCLA, studied over 25,000 students for more than ten years. He discovered that students highly involved in arts programs fare better in other subjects too. Catterall's study also shows that students from low-income families who participate in the arts are more likely to do better academically than those who do not.[3]

The John Eliot School in Needham, Massachusetts, is a case in point. With the same budget as that of other schools in Needham and the same professional staffing — 13 full-time teachers and 13 part-time professionals for 306 students — it has half-time music and art teachers. In addition, Principal Miriam Kronish makes good use of artists-in-residence: two years ago the poet was so effective in training the teachers that everyone is still writing poetry. Three-quarters of the students take instrumental lessons; all of them sing in the fourth and fifth grades. "The arts," said the principal, "make everything personal," and students are not afraid of taking risks.[1]

What I Say

There were so many experts screaming, "Arts programs matter," that I knew I had to do something. Armed with the expert testimonials, I went to the school principal. Remembering from my childhood that she was "the pal" in princi*pal*, I asked her what we could do.

"Budget cuts, No Child Left Behind, understaffed, overworked teachers," was her disappointing answer. I realized it was time for parents to step up.

Who Am I, Anyway?

I run a national theatre program for teens called Showdown. For five years I've been in the child trenches, helping kids through theatre. I've seen firsthand what it can do.

In addition to that, Flip Kobler, my husband and writing partner, and I have written many animated films for Disney: *Lion King II*, *Beauty and the Beast: The Enchanted Christmas*, and lots of other movies. Heck, we were on staff there for over five years.

I've had six young adult plays published with Pioneer Drama Service, Inc., plus a few adult pieces with Samuel French, and another with Dramatic Publishing. All in all, you could say the arts consume a lot of my life.

Why This Book?

PLAYdate is based on my experiences teaching theatre arts. It's for parents and educators like you who have little time or money, but lots of passion for kids and a willing heart.

Step by step, week by week, *PLAYdate* will help you travel this exhausting, exhilarating, magical world of theatre with your child. Like the captain of a very unusual ship, you'll journey with your crew. While your eager young artists learn how to project, you, the exhausted old parent or educator, will learn when it's time to buy a bucket of Ben and Jerry's. Children will learn theatre games, you will learn theatre trivia, bits of gossip, and notable quotes. For example, Sidonie-Gabrielle Colette's quote, "You will do foolish things, but do them with enthusiasm," will keep you and everyone else having fun right up to opening night.

So How Does This Book Work?

PLAYdate is broken down into twelve chapters. Each chapter builds on the last. In the first chapter, you'll meet your kids and play a whole bunch of kid-tested-and-approved games with them. From there, you'll pick out a show. For the creative minded — or those who think locks of gray hair actually make them look distinguished — you'll write a play with the kids. But no worries for those who are the "She's got to be kidding, I have no time for this" parent or educator, you'll be given great resources for finding a written show. I've even thrown in a couple I've used in the past to make it really easy. You'll then travel through rehearsals. You will learn the "art" of recruiting other parent volunteers, because nobody should have this much fun and not share it. Simple set, prop, and costume making will also be covered; lots of facts, forms, and fun will keep you on your path to opening night. In addition, anecdotes will reassure you that you haven't lost your mind … yet.

The Chapters' Inside Skinny

Within each chapter there are a few items to keep you enjoying your journey from page to stage.

TLC Tips

Don't be alarmed. Don't pass go. Don't collect $200. But along the way you are going to need some self-care. The little darlings — and their mommies and daddies — can take a toll on your sanity. TLC Tips are just as they say — little tips from me to you to keep a smile on your face and a song in your heart.

Like Cindy's TLC Tip #27 (recommended after getting twenty-three third graders to sing at the same time).

Cindy's TLC Tip #27

Ben and Jerry have a new version of Phish Food. Buy the new flavor with the little white chocolate cows and the original. Do a taste test, preferably in your car where you don't have to share. Don't worry about the calories. The acid from your pending ulcer will burn them right up.

But then there are also some serious tips, like Cindy's TLC Tip #39C (recommended after completing your first read-through).

Cindy's TLC Tip #39C

If you are a parent director, take you and your little fella out for a treat. Listen to him or her prattle on about the pending show. Savor their excitement — and yours. If you're a teacher director, it's time for a treat. Something ooey-gooey. And while you eat, look back at the work you've done and savor the excitement of your group of little guys. You're amazing.

Cindy's View of the World

These are little bits of things I've learned. Hopefully, they'll help you survive, I mean, enjoy this nutty path you're about to walk.

Cindy's View of the World #19

Grown-ups are little kids in big bodies. We need playtime and treats and mini-parades as much as the little ones. So get in there and play, too. Not only will they love you more for it, but you'll have more fun.

Once Upon a Time in Cindyland ...

These are my anecdotes, my stories from deep inside the trenches of Hollywood and theatre. Hopefully, my journey will give you a perspective that will make you realize you're exactly where you need to be. And if you're not, just move one foot to the left or right and you'll be there.

Trivia Time

I don't know how much clearer I can make this. It's trivia. I put this in for those people who like to go to parties and say things like, **"Did you know Terrance Winter (an executive producer for *Sopranos*) posed as his own agent to get his first script sold?"** Or **"Did you know the guy who wrote *High School Musical* was in his fifties when he sold that script to Disney?"**

It's a Wrap

This might be used as a review of what you've learned because it's really complicated and you were probably going to bed when you read the chapter and won't remember it, so I want to make it as easy for you as possible. Or it could be just a prep for the following week. Either way, it's to simplify your life.

I haven't included all of these subheadings in every chapter, so don't worry if you don't see one. But you'll find that most do.

You Rock!

You picked up this book because you have high hopes for your child or class. You want to see them live in a better world. Don't let this be a coffee table book. Use it. Live it. Let the corners get worn with overuse, let the pages become jelly-stained from the hands of your little one or class looking through it with you.

You can do this. You can have fun. You can make a difference. And if all that isn't reason enough to put on a theatre arts program, there's the way cool book of stick figure drawings you're bound to get, the construction paper card with your name misspelled, and the gazillion hugs of appreciation for giving your child and class more fun than they've ever had in school before.

Ready?

Let's go.

Notes

1. Fulbright, Harriet M. "The Arts At the Heart of Learning." 1997. New Horizons for Learning. Apr. 2008 <http://www.newhorizons.org/strategies/arts/cabc/fulbright.htm

2. Sun, Ping-Yun. "Online Resources for Theatre Education. ERIC Digest." Dec. 2001. ERIC. Apr. 2008 <http://www.ericdigests.org/2002-2/theatre.htm>.

3. Hartman, Carl. "Arts May Improve Student's Grade." Educational Cyber Playground. Apr. 2008 <http://www.edu-cyberpg.com/music/carl.html>.

Chapter One

Meet and Greet

"Hiiii Mrs. Marcus, thank you for coming to class."

Once Upon a Time in Cindyland ...

Thump. Thump. *Thummmmp!* My heart was beating so hard, I thought it was going to rip right through my rib cage. I could just see it. The pounding mass of red gelatin would bounce onto the floor, thrilling my son and every other third grade boy in that class. "Ooooh it's your mom's heart, cool!" Score one for me. I've made my kid really popular, but I've lost my heart. Oh boy, talk about your metaphors. Is that what I'm in for today?

It's my first day in front of the firing squad of kids. And I'm going to teach them how to put on a play. For the next however many weeks it takes, I will be coming in with my trusty assistant, Annie, to guide the kids from page to stage. This seemed like a good idea when Mr. Flores first approached me and asked me to do this. But then again, I thought the new Coke was yummy and the grapefruit diet would work.

"So what do you have for us?" Mr. Flores asks.

I stare out at the children's eager little faces. Twenty-two sets of eyes gaze back at me. I think, "Run! There's still time. Save yourself!" Unfortunately, my feet do not cooperate with my brain and I remain planted. "We're going to be putting on a play," I gulp.

I look at the clock. That took ten seconds. I realize I have another hour, fourteen minutes, and fifty seconds to fill. Thump. Tick. Thump. Tick. The ticking of the clock has now joined the thumping of my heart. Disaster looms.

"What's a play?" asks one of the children.

"A play?" I repeat.

And my son, bless his little heart, raises his hand, but doesn't wait for me to call on him and says, "Well a play is when we all get to get up and pretend to be different people and it's really fun."

In the sea of faces, I see a smile or two. There's a twinkle of hope in their eyes — or maybe it's just gas — but at this point, I'll take any sign that this grand experiment might turn out OK.

And so I began what was one of the most challenging, frustrating, joyful, and rewarding experiences of my mommyhood. I took it one day at a time. Each week I came in prepped and ready, but willing to revamp if need be. Some of the days were awful. I knew this because the little guys said things to me like, "That was awful." But most days I did OK. And you will, too. No, you'll be great.

Cindy's View of the World #1

Let's face it, we're all little children — some of us reside in big bodies, some of us in small, grass-stained frames — and we all want to have fun and be liked. Remember that they want you to do a good job and to be fun and wonderful as much as you do. They're on your side.

OK, how do you win over those little rapscallions while inspiring their imagination, and still enjoy the journey yourself?

Theatre Games

"For every job that must be done there is an element of fun. And snap the job's a game."* **(Who said that? I'll give you a hint: she flies using an umbrella.)**

Theatre games are interactive, imagination-building exercises you do with the kids. They're not only fun for the little guys, but they learn, and you do, too! Repeat after me, "Theatre games are my friend." And they are.

If the children get too unruly and start hanging from the rafters, do a game — they'll calm down and focus immediately. If the kids are bored, do a game. If the kids are behaving and they need a reward, do a game. If you need a break, do a game. And don't worry about repeating games. Children love repetition — except when you ask them to brush their teeth or clean their room, then it doesn't matter.

Cindy's View of the World #2B

Don't stand by on the sidelines. Always, always play with them. This puts you in the trenches right beside them. If they see you doing everything you ask them to do, they will learn that you are one of them. And this will come in way handy when you get into dress rehearsals and you're screaming like a banshee to get their attention. You'll have played with them so much, they will forgive your shortcomings.

So now the question is, which games do you play?

The Name Game

I like to start with this.

Everyone sits in his or her classroom seat. You use the area by the chalkboard as your "stage." If you're lucky enough to be sitting in your Multi-Purpose Room (MPR) or a theatre, then everyone sits out in the audience. Start by asking for volunteers. There are usually one or two hams in every group, thank goodness. Ask them to go up on stage, one at a time, and say their name and their favorite dessert. That's it. Everyone must get up and do this. You too!

Now, what I like to do is draw the kids out. I ask them about their favorite ooey-gooey treat. Do you like nuts on it? Do you prefer your pie with cheese or ice cream? What kind, vanilla or chocolate? This may seem like I'm just a sweetaholic — OK, I confess, maybe I am — but truth be told, by asking these children questions about something they enjoy, you learn a great deal about them. Who is afraid to speak? Who is loud? Who can build on their imagination? All of these little tidbits of information will come in handy as you move through this process. And it's fun. I know, I know, doesn't seem like a game, does it? But it is.

Oh, and by the by, you don't just have to have the kids say their favorite dessert; there's also their favorite thing to do, favorite food, or movie, or book, or color. The list is endless. You can even let them choose.

The Name Game, the Sequel

This particular game builds memory skills. Everyone stands or sits in a big circle. You start with the child next to you. He or she will say their name and then something they like to do. Now go to the kid next to him or her. That child will say the first child's name and what that child likes to do; he or she will add their name and their favorite thing to do. It's time to go to the third child. This little one relays the information of child one and two then adds his or her brand of info. On and on we go around the circle until we get to you. You need to be the last person in the circle. You then say all the names plus your special whatever.

Guess what? You've not only learned the names of the children and what they like to do, but who has a good memory, which is awesome to know when you get to casting. You want to give the "larger" parts to the kids who can handle the memorizing.

From here on, you choose whatever order and whenever you want to do the games. I suggest doing at least one each time you come into the classroom.

Machines

Machines are an awesome post-recess kind of a game because the kids get a chance to get out all those final oogly googlies before sitting down and getting to work.

That child will go up to the "stage" and perform a simple motion of some kind. (Choose a child to start.) Maybe they swing their arms up and down. Or they can stomp their feet. Or they bend over and then stand up. It should be something they can repeat easily. The rest of the children are then directed to go up one at a time and they must connect with the child next to them in some way. Maybe this little shaver is standing with his or her arms outstretched like a giant T and swiveling at the waist. He or she must coordinate their timing so their arms swing over the kid next to him or her while they are bending over. Keep going until all the children have added their movement. That's it. Fun, huh?

Guess what you accomplished with this little game? You showed them how to work together. You helped to create an ensemble.

Part Deux: Same game, each child adds a sound. The sounds and the movement must be easy to repeat and very simple. That's it. Keep it going until you have a cacophony of noise and movement.

Part Trois: Same game, each child does an emotional noise instead. They can say, "ha ha," or "wah," or "urgh!" On and on it goes. Again, the kids must create off of the child before them.

Part Quatre: This is for when the little people have been cast. Ask them to do the machine, but the movement must represent their character. When we did our play, *The Queen's New Heater*, the kid who played the writer did a crying noise and then jumped up and down, because no one ever listened to his character and he was always distraught. The girl playing the Queen waved her arm a little and said, "Hello."

Air Guitar

This is a fun way to get the kids loosened up. All you do is tell them to scatter around the room or stage and have them play air guitar. You can play music if you like, or you can have their imaginations play the music. It's really simple and it gives you a chance to rock out too! Plus, it lets you see which kids aren't shy and which are willing to ham it up.

The air guitar game is a great way to let our imaginations get carried away while loosening up for rehearsal.

Props

For this, you're going to need to bring in a piece of clothing or a prop of some kind. Make sure it's old and not something you care about, like grandma's grand diamond tiara. Start with a volunteer. Have the child go up on "stage" and create a character using the costume. No sound. They have to do this silently. And then we get to guess who they are. So for example, you bring in a scarf, which can become Superman's cape, an old babushka, or an expensive wrap. A pen can be a cigar, a sword, or an alien's antennae. You get the idea. Encourage each child to get up. Even if they stare at you with their wide baby blues and tell you, "I can't think of anything," don't let them get away with that. Get up with them. Have the other kids brainstorm. Whatever it takes to make sure each child gets their moment on stage.

Cindy's View of the World #900

Remember, there is no wrong when the children are playing games. Every idea is a good one as long as it stays within the rules you've set up. Make sure to tell them so. Our goal here is to build their confidence, make it as safe as possible for them to take creative risks. You too! And if no one tells you how good your apple core or alien or old woman was, I will. Wow! That was the juiciest core, the scariest alien, and the prettiest old woman I've ever seen. Keep it up.

Zip, Zap, Zop

Yes, that's what I said, Zip, Zap, Zop. This is a game of focus. And it's a little challenging to explain so bear with me. But it's fun. And the kids love it. Let me repeat, *love it!*

Have all the little tykes stand in a circle. One person quickly claps and points at someone while saying "zip." The person who received the "zip" then claps and points at another while saying "zap." That person then claps and points to someone while saying "zop." The pattern continues, "zip, zap, zop, zip, zap, zop ..."

It takes a while to get into the rhythm of the game. Don't give up. Eventually, the group will go lightning-quick and the game will get really fun. This game usually ends up in titters, guffaws, and sometimes hysterics. That's because you have to focus so intently. You don't want to be zopped and not have been paying attention. Everyone must watch everything that is going on so you'll see twenty-two pair of eyes riveted to the imaginary zips, zaps, zops as they bounce around the ring. If you can, step out of the circle and watch these eager little eyes focus as if doing brain surgery.

Take a Look

This is a game of observation. Have everyone stand in two lines, making sure each person has a partner to look at. Now, ask each person to silently study their partner. Give them about thirty seconds. Ask them to notice what their partner is wearing, how they've done their hair, whatever. This is a silent game, so shhhh! Now have everyone turn their backs to each other and change three things about the way they look. Maybe they take off a shoe or pull their hair up or unbutton a button or two, roll up a sleeve, turn a pocket inside-out. Give them twenty seconds or less to do this. Now everyone turns back around. Partners have to figure out what's different. Ask everyone to share their observation. You can continue to do this as many times as you like, having them face each other and then turn around each time, asking them to change more things. Remember to remind them to keep it clean.

It's a Wrap!

Well, hoo-ha! You did it. You made it through your first day and you actually had fun — I hope.

What you accomplished today:

• You learned the names of all the kids.

• You now know those six or seven children who will project, memorize, and have little or no stage fright.

• You've made friends with twenty or so little people.

• You're a hero because you turned an ordinary day into something magical.

Cindy's TLC Tip #1

You deserve a treat. What *do* you like? Is it ice cream? Starbucks' mocha? Is it a yummy cinnamon scone? If you're a parent, take you and your little one out after school today and celebrate. Listen to him or her talk about this and that and what you did today. If you're a teacher director, go out after school today and celebrate. We who have walked a mile in your shoes salute you. Can you see us? Yay for you! Cherish this moment. But trust me, there are many more to come.

Trivia Time

* **"For every job that must be done ... " is a quote from *Mary Poppins*, but you knew that, right?**

Once Upon a Time in Cindyland ...

As I look back on that first day with the kids, I wonder why I was so terrified. After all, I've dined with celebs and worked with stars. I remember when my husband, Flip, and I flew to New York to record Ernie Sabella and Nathan Lane for *Lion King II*. Ernie and Nathan were starring in *A Funny Thing Happened on the Way to the Forum*. Ernie got us front row tickets for our first night in town. The show rocked! I think Ernie actually even winked at us when he took a bow.

OK, so now the show is over and Ernie, who we'd just barely met before the show started, says, "You wanna walk on the boards?" For a couple of starry-eyed kids who'd dreamed of Broadway most of their lives, this was a dream come true. So there we are, walking on a Broadway stage, staring out at the empty seats. Wow! Flip even tried, "To be or not to be." Surprisingly, no producers came out of the rain to offer us a contract, but hey, it was still an awesome moment. Nathan had a cold so he begged off, but Ernie invited us to Sardi's for dinner. Sardi's? Us! Wow! Off we go and as we're leaving the theatre, there's this mob of high school kids milling around a bus waiting for their return trip to Peoria. As we pass, Ernie goes into his Pumba mode and belts, "Hakuna Matata." It took about three seconds for him to be mobbed by the crowd, begging for him to sign autographs on shirts, the soles of their shoes, they'da had him tattoo it on to their tongues if they had a needle. But here's the cool part — in the midst of all of this, Ernie hands his pen to me and tells the crowd, "You want to get *these guys'* autographs. They wrote the sequel."

So why on earth was I so terrified of facing my son's third grade class? Maybe it's because I wanted to make a difference in a profound way. Or maybe it's because Finn is still that age when I can be a hero. In just a few more years, I will be the enemy. I will be the one who doesn't get it, who hates his music, and thinks he needs a haircut. But right now, I'm da bomb. And I wanted to hold that place in his heart a few minutes longer.

Chapter Two

Choosing the Play

"What play are we doing, huh? Huh? What play?"

"The play's the thing." — **The Bard** *

How to Find a Play

"Ye Ha!" You made it through your first meet and greet, you know who your kids are — sort of. You have a sense of what they can and can't do — kind of. It's now time to pick the show.

Teachers

Some teachers are magical beings. They can pull rabbits out of hats, **spin straw into gold** * * — **OK, they can't do that, but they'd know in which story you'd find that character.**

Students have a mandate that must be met. Depending on the time of year, what standards they're attempting to meet, what other classes they are studying, and how tired they are, your play can help teachers and students meet that. Maybe it's February, and the little people are studying presidents. Your show can be about Honest Abe. Or maybe they're studying fairy tales. Your play can be a spin on Cinderella.

Teachers also have access to countless stories they've always thought would make great plays. You can adapt a tale. But for those of you who are less intrepid and don't want to face writing a show, teachers know all kinds of plays already written that are totally school appropriate.

Libraries

Yes, this is obvious. But did you know there are all kinds of libraries?

You can go to the library down the street with the lovely librarian and ask her about finding a play for your little ones. She'll guide you to the right section. She may also have a personal recommendation or two.

Did you also know there are publishers out there with libraries of shows? Contemporary Drama Service, Pioneer Drama Service, and Dramatic Publishing Company — on and on it goes. Now, to perform their plays, you will have to pay for rights. What this means is that to use these plays, you have to pay a fee — this is the time when bake sales and car washes usually dance across your vision. But the fee is usually minimal and you get the added benefit of working with a proven commodity.

Internet

Type "plays for children" in a search engine on the internet and see what comes up. Did you know there are even public domain versions of Shakespeare junior? Public domain means the play doesn't cost you a dime to adapt or perform because of ... well ... a lot of legal mumbo jumbo that you can investigate if you want. Shakespeare junior is a website and a wonderful resource. It's fun to travel through and learn neat things, but it won't give you a usable play. Their website is Shakespearejr.com.

You can go to Charles and Mary Lamb's website called Tales from Shakespeare (For Children) and find public domain Shakespeare in story format. It's terribly usable, you just need to convert the "story" format to script format and you're good to go. That website is http://shakespeare.palomar.edu /lambtales/LAMBTALE.HTM. I used this for our little guy production of *A Midsummer Night's Dream* and it came out really cute.

There is also www.Shakespeare-literature.com. Here you can learn a little about Shakespeare. It also has his plays to read, which include a synopsis. You can use a play's synopsis to help adapt your own version, similar to what you can do at Tales from Shakespeare.

Also, there's the Folger Shakespeare Library. It's an awesome resource and there are workshops for teachers and kids. You can find them at Folger.edu. They, too, have books, but they charge for them.

Moliére, Dickens, Brothers Grimm, Hans Christian Andersen, and Greek tragedies are also public domain and therefore free for you to adapt and use.

Finally, there are those stories from your childhood. Special books your mom read to you. Or maybe there's a tale handed down about your grandfather who escaped from the pogroms of Russia — no, wait, that's a story handed down to me, but you can use it. Just make sure that if you use a book, the rights are available. In other words, clear it with the author, get his or her OK that you can use his or her book. Authors are happy to share their stories if they know it's for kids.

OK, so we've seen there's no shortage of places to find our source material. But what are your parameters? What kind of show do you choose?

What to Look For in a Play

A Large Cast

Choose a show with a large cast. You want to make sure you have a part for each child. Even if all they say is one word, it's important that each little person get their moment. Remember, you're doing this for the kids and nothing builds self-confidence more than getting up in front of an audience and having a moment to shine.

Once Upon a Time in Cindyland ...

We had a little girl in our first summer teen camp in Florida. I'll call her my Random Princess, because that's who she became. Anyway, Random Princess rarely spoke above a whisper. Really, you couldn't hear her five inches away. She was shy and withdrawn. I don't think I saw her smile once, and no one was sure she even had teeth. But our camp mandate was that every kid has a role, so we had to find a place for her in one of the shows. I put her in our comedy. Disaster. I tried making her my assistant director, hoping that would open her up. Disaster. Finally, I cast her in a role as one of our Greek Chorus. Well, this group of kids had to do some stage combat. And lo and behold! Random Princess had a gift for sword fighting. Somewhere in her family there was a martial arts teacher. I'm telling you, when I saw that, the clouds parted and I heard heavenly music. I had an opening with her — a place to make her shine. Random Princess became my combat captain; she would teach the other kids how to fight. Long story made short — too late, I know — Random Princess transformed after that show. She came back the following summer with a voice to die for and we cast her as our romantic lead in the comedy. And she continues to blossom and grow. (And does have great dental work, by the way.)

Every Child Must Have a Moment

Let's take off the director's hat and put on the parental sombrero. Parents want to see their kid up on stage so they can take lots and lots of pictures that they will shove into a drawer and probably never look at again. No matter. Their pumpkin needs his or her moment.

Got it? Now, what if you can't find a show with lots of parts? Then you expand the roles you have. Three narrators can become six. With one prince, you can add his sidekick, his conscience, his horse, his squire — on and on it goes. The kids are actually great at helping come up with new characters once you get the ball rolling.

I say it again: every child gets a moment. *Every child.*

A Simple Set

A set is the backdrop of your show. Usually that means: some flats, those large walls in the background, a few pieces of furniture, and a prop or two.

It is preferable your play take place in one location.

I know we all have grandiose dreams that our little show will somehow become the next *Les Miserables* or *Phantom of the Opera*, but in reality you're in a school with a limited budget and less time. And honestly, the parents are there to see their children; they'd be happy watching them on a pile of phone books. For your sanity and everyone else around, think simple. Think suggestive:

a library is really only one shelf of books, a castle is one big fancy chair painted gold, a bedroom is a mirror or a dressing table. So when deciding upon your play, keep your set in mind.

Less Is More

Good rule of thumb, figure every page in your script will run about a minute on stage, give or take how well the little darlings remember their lines. I suggest you keep your show to less than fifteen pages. That's long enough so the kids feel like they did something, but short enough for you to keep yourself from pulling out all your hair. A few strands, even a clump will probably leave your skull by the end and will grow back, but much more than that and you'll scare the smaller children.

Know Your Company

Not the couple you're having over for dinner this Saturday night, silly. I'm talking about your company of actors, your kids. Choose a show that they can do successfully. If you have thirty kindergarteners and five third graders, you probably want to stay away from Shakespeare. Keep it simple. Aim for basic dialogue and lots of character groups so memorizing lines doesn't become a challenge. Remember, the wee little ones can get easily overwhelmed. If you have a passel of savvy sixth graders, you can take on a more challenging piece, maybe one that incorporates a monologue or two. *Monologues* are paragraphs of lines delivered by one person, think Hamlet's "To be or not to be."

What Speaks to You?

"There is a vitality, a life force, an energy, a quickening, that is translated through you into action, and because there is only one of you in all time, this expression is unique. And if you block it, it will never exist through any other medium and will be lost."

— Martha Graham

You are the captain of this boat, the admiral, the head dude, and you have to keep it going through some pretty rocky waters. It will be your enthusiasm for this play that will get your cranky darlings over the rough humps and keep your volunteers from abandoning ship. Choose a show that you love. You're going to be living with it for the next ten to fifteen weeks and you want to enjoy it. Funny thing about fun, it's infectious. So pick something that speaks to you.

Cindy's TLC Tip #6

Make sure to always keep a book around that you're reading for pleasure. I tend to prefer legal thrillers, but you may like historical romances, biographies, or tech manuals. It doesn't matter. Reading for the sake of reading calms the mind, and keeps your passion for literature alive.

So this is all well and good if you have a lot of time or you like doing this kind of research. But what if you don't? I have a solution for you, too.

A Ready Made Play

It's my gift to you. We wrote *The Five Chinese Brothers* based on the old Chinese folk tale. Our challenge with this particular show was that we had loads of children of varying ages. We had to make sure that no line was too long or conceptually too hard to understand. The humor had to be accessible for kids, yet enjoyable for parents. Not an easy task. However, I'm happy to report that this show was done for happy mommies and daddies in St. Pete, Florida. So it's kid tested and audience approved.

The Five Chinese Brothers
By Flip Kobler and Cindy Marcus (that's me!)

(Lights up on a blank stage. Leave it blank because it's easy to do that as a set. The S group and T group come rushing on. The T group carries a ball.)

SUSIE: Hey, give it back.

TOMMY: No.

STEVIE: It's ours.

TOMMY: No.

SAMMY: Yes.

TERRY: It belongs to us.

SUSIE: No, it doesn't.

TABBY: Does too.

STEVIE: Does not. It belongs to the school.

SAMMY: That's government property.

TERRY: Well if it's government stuff, then it's not yours.

TABBY: Stealing from the government is a crime. Unless you work there.

SUSIE: We didn't steal it.

TOMMY: Then it's not yours.

STEVIE: It's more ours than it is yours.

TOMMY: No.

SUSIE: We were playing with it.

TABBY: And now we are.

SAMMY: Well you guys are just big banana heads.

TERRY, TABBY, and TOMMY: Ooooh.

NARRATOR 1: *(Entering with NARRATOR 2)* What's going on here?

TABBY: They're calling us fruit-based names.

STEVIE: No, we didn't.

TERRY: Did too. Did too.

TOMMY: Liar.

TABBY: Your pants are on fire.

NARRATOR 1: Tell me what happened. (*Both groups talking over each other.*)

NARRATOR 2: One at a time. (*Both groups talking over each other again.*)

NARRATOR 1: OK. Easy. You tell me what happened.

SUSIE: We were playing ball and having lots of fun.

STEVIE: Not lots of fun.

SUSIE: Well we were having some fun.

SAMMY: I was bored.

SUSIE: And they came by and took the ball. We want it back.

TOMMY: Can't have it.

NARRATOR 1: Is that what happened?

SUSIE: You don't have to ask them. I just told you what happened.

NARRATOR 2: There are two sides to every story.

SAMMY: Not this one.

NARRATOR 2: Two sides to *every* story.

SUSIE: I just told you what happened. Why don't you ever believe me? It's the truth.

NARRATOR 3: (*Entering and talking to the audience*) Hello, ladies and gentlemen. Hi, mom! (*Waves to his or her mom.*) We here at _____ (*insert your school name*) feel there are two sides to every story. And since this is not a court of law but a theatre, it would be in our best interest to demonstrate this with the use of a parable.

TOMMY: I don't want to be a parable.

SUSIE: What are parables?

TOMMY: It's like two cows.

NARRATOR 3: A parable is a story. And you don't get to be part of this one.

TABBY: Why not?

SAMMY: Yeah, that's not fair.

NARRATOR 3: Because this one happened a long time ago. Before you were born.

TABBY: We could still be in it.

NARRATOR 3: In China.

TABBY: Oh.

NARRATOR 3: Now sit and I'll tell you the story. (*The T group and the S group gather on the edge of the stage and listen. Chinese music sneaks up. The narrators gather on the apron.*)

NARRATOR 1: Once upon a time in ancient China, there lived five Chinese brothers who looked exactly alike. (*FIVE BROTHERS march out and stand in a line. They don't look anything alike and we're not even sure they're all boys.*)

NARRATOR 2: They don't look that much alike.

NARRATOR 1: This is dumb. They look totally different. And some are

girls. (*The BROTHERS all put on skull caps with long braids down the back.*) **Ahhhh. Identical.**

NARRATOR 2: **Spooky.**

NARRATOR 1: **No one could ever tell them apart.**

NARRATOR 2: **Not without a DNA test. Twins. Carbon copies. Perfect Xeroxes.**

NARRATOR 3: **They get it. Each brother had a unique skill.** (*DING starts doing ninja moves. LING works a yo-yo. PING jumps rope. TING does a yoga pose. ZING dances old school.*) **Even more unique than this.** (*To the XINGS*) **Stop it.**

NARRATOR 1: **The first brother, Ding, could hold the entire sea in his mouth.** (*DING bows.*)

NARRATOR 2: **The second brother, Ling, had a neck made of iron.** (*LING raises his hands like a champ.*)

NARRATOR 3: **Ping had legs that could stretch and stretch.** (*PING shakes his Jell-o legs.*) **Ting could not be burned.** (*TING licks his thumb and puts it on his hip and makes a sizzling noise.*)

NARRATOR 1: **And Zing could hold his breath forever.** (*Zing gulps air and waves to the crowd.*) **And they all lived with their loving mother in a village by the sea.** (*MOMMA XING comes out and bows to the crowd.*)

NARRATOR 2: **Now every morning, Ding would go fishing.** (*DING crosses the stage with a fishing pole over his shoulder.*) **And every day he would return with a load of exotic and expensive fish.** (*The cast, or anybody we can use as villagers, "ooooh" and "ahhhh" as DING comes back on with a pole loaded with construction paper fish.*)

NARRATOR 3: **He sold his fish and made a good living for Momma and his brothers. But one day, some other fishermen begged him to share his secret for catching fish.** (*TROUT, MACKEREL, and SQUID enter. They run to DING.*)

TROUT: **Ding. Hey, Ding. Will you teach us your secret of fishing?**

DING: **I am humbly sorry, I must say no.**

MACKEREL: **Please, oh please. We just gotta know.**

DING: **It is a family secret. I must decline.**

SQUID: **But my family is starving.**

DING: **Starving?**

SQUID: **We haven't eaten in weeks.**

TROUT: **Our mom has us on a wonton diet. Every night we have wonton something to eat.**

DING: **Is this true?** (*FISHERMEN nod.*) **Alright. Meet me at the seashore at dawn tomorrow.**

NARRATOR 3: **So the three fishermen went to bed.** (*They lay down and do a Three Stooges snore for two seconds.*) **And were up bright and early the next day.** (*The FISHERMEN leap to their feet.*) **And met Ding on the seashore.**

DING: **I can help you get all the fish you desire. But only if you follow** my rules exactly.

TROUT: We will.

DING: You must promise.

TROUT: We promise.

DING: This is very important.

TROUT: Yeah, yeah, you gonna help us or yak all day?

DING: When I wave my arms like this, *(Demonstrates)* you must come right back to me.

TROUT: OK.

DING: Right back. Instantly.

TROUT: Got it.

DING: What do you do when I wave my arms like this?

TROUT: Run back to you, what are we, stupid?

DING: I wave —

TROUT: And we come. Yeesh. Get a move on, Ding.

DING: Alright. Watch carefully. *(DING kneels and mimes drinking from the sea.)*

NARRATOR 2: So Ding did what he does. He swallowed the entire sea. Sucked that puppy dry.

FISHERMEN: Whoa.

NARRATOR 2: Until there was no water left at all and the sea bed was full of flopping fish.

SQUID: OK, you gotta admit, that's cool.

TROUT: Let's go fishing.

NARRATOR 1: So the fishermen ran into the sea and collected all the fish they could carry. But it wasn't long before *(DING is waving his arms like crazy)* Ding could no longer hold the sea.

MACKEREL: Hey, we gotta go.

SQUID: Trout, come on. *(MACKEREL and SQUID stand next to DING.)*

TROUT: In a minute.

MACKEREL: *(DING is leaping, waving, and grunting.)* I don't think he has a minute.

TROUT: I'm not done.

SQUID: We already have more than we can eat.

TROUT: Then we can sell 'em.

DING: *(Grunts.)* Oof. Oh. Yanngh.

SQUID: I don't think he can hold it.

TROUT: He's just trying to keep us from getting rich like him.

MACKEREL: You think?

TROUT: Yah. He's selfish.

NARRATOR 3: But Ding wasn't being selfish. The sea had to come back and he simply couldn't hold it anymore. *(DING mimes spitting huge.)* The sea flooded back.

MACKEREL and SQUID: *Trout!*

NARRATOR 3: But Trout hadn't listened. Hadn't fulfilled his promise. And was lost beneath the waves. (*MACKEREL and SQUID stand in shock. DING sinks to his knees and cries.*)

DING: What have I done?

NARRATOR 2: Mackerel and Squid were cheesed off over the loss of their friend and they took Ding to see the judge. (*MACKEREL and SQUID grab DING's arms and lead him Off-stage while the set changes. A large chair is placed in center where the JUDGE sits. A crowd gathers. MACKEREL and SQUID kneel on either side of the JUDGE. DING is on his knees before him.*)

NARRATOR 1: Where they told their side of the story.

MACKEREL: And then he just spit back the sea.

JUDGE: He gave you no warning?

SQUID: None. Zero. Zip.

JUDGE: That is barbaric.

MACKEREL: I think he was jealous that Trout was a better fisherman than he was.

JUDGE: Was anyone else there to see this?

MACKEREL: No, just me and Squid.

DING: Your honor, please.

JUDGE: Enough out of you.

DING: Please, sir, I haven't told my side of the story.

JUDGE: Your side does not matter. I have two stories here. It is two against one, whatever you say. For this heartless crime, Ding, I sentence you to have your head cut off in the morning. (*The crowd cheers. MACKEREL and SQUID high five.*)

DING: But your honor —

JUDGE: No more. Take him away.

NARRATOR 1: So they took Ding away and kept him under guard for the night. (*The chair is taken Off-stage and now the stage is blank.*) That night, Mamma Xing and her sons come to visit Ding. (*MAMMA XING and the BROTHERS enter and surround the guards.*)

MOMMA XING: I am here to see my son. (*The guards bow and step back a few paces.*) Ding, did you do this thing?

DING: Momma, I waved. I tried to warn him to come back.

MOMMA XING: What did the judge say to this?

DING: He wouldn't hear my side.

MOMMA XING: Then this is not justice, and we do not obey. Group hug. (*THEY huddle together. Chinese music plays. When they part, DING leaves with the family and LING stays behind.*)

NARRATOR 2: That night, Ding left with his family and his brother Ling took his place. The next morning the crowd gathered for the execution. (*CROWD enters with a chopping block. EXECUTIONER enters. LING is led in and placed on the block.*)

JUDGE: Executioner, do your duty. (*EXECUTIONER raises his cardboard axe and chops. We hear a metallic* ding. *LING smiles. The crowd gasps. The EXECUTIONER tries again.* Ding. *And again.* Ding. *Soon he's hacking like crazy until he drops the axe and is exhausted.)*

JUDGE: What magic is this?

LING: No magic, your honor. Perhaps justice is not served. If you would only hear my tale —

JUDGE: I will not be taken by lies, trickster. I sentence you to be drowned at dawn.

NARRATOR 1: So the guards took Ling away for the night and again, Momma Xing and her sons came to visit. *(Stage clears.)*

MOMMA XING: What did the judge say?

LING: He would not hear my side.

MOMMA XING: Then this is not justice and we do not obey. Group hug. Huggies for everyone. *(Again, THEY close in for a group hug. When they pull back, LING leaves with the group and PING stays behind.)* **Goodnight, Ling.**

LING: *(From the group)* **Goodnight Momma — Oooof.** *(TING slaps the back of his head.)*

PING: Goodnight, Momma.

NARRATOR 3: The next morning the crowd had gathered at the sea. Ping was placed in a boat and rowed out to the middle of the sea. *(This can be mimed or use a cardboard cutout boat.)* **And thrown over the side.** *(The CROWD cheers. Two people with a blue bed sheet hold it up and wave it like the waves. PING ducks behind it. The crowd cheers louder.)*

NARRATOR 1: But Ping could stretch and stretch his legs. Which he did. *(Now someone brings a stepladder in from the wings and sets it center stage. The two holding the bed sheet unfold it so it hides the entire ladder. Chinese music plays. A moment later, PING's head pops up above the sheet. The CROWD gasps.)*

JUDGE: This Ding cannot be drowned.

MACKEREL: Maybe his name is Bob.

SQUID: Yeah. Or Floaty.

MACKEREL: Floaty? Bob is funny. Yours is just lame.

JUDGE: *(Shouting to PING's floating head)* **If you will not drown, then you will be burned at the stake ... In the morning.**

SQUID: Why not just do it now?

JUDGE: Always in the morning. And I have a Tai Chi class in fifteen minutes. *(The stage is cleared.)*

NARRATOR 2: So once again the guards took Ping away, and once again Momma and her sons came to visit.

MOMMA XING: Did he —

PING: Nope.

MOMMA XING: Fine. Group hug. *(They ALL hug.)*

NARRATOR 2: And you can pretty much guess what happened. *(TING is left in PING's place.)* **The next day the crowd had gathered for the burning.** *(A large pole like a PVC pipe or carpet tube is center stage. TING* *is led in and tied to it. Several of the CROWD are in the yoga child's pose around the pole. They carry red or yellow scarves in each hand.)*

JUDGE: Ding, I sentence you to be burned. *(Slowly, the kids in the yoga pose wave the scarves like flames. Higher, faster. Soon they're on their knees, then standing, then dancing as the fire goes wild. Chinese fire music plays. Through it all TING just smiles.)*

JUDGE: He's not burning.

MACKEREL: Maybe his name is Stew.

SQUID: Yeah, or Char.

MACKEREL: Char? Really?

SQUID: Sorry.

TING: Can somebody get me a sweater. I'm feeling a little drafty.

JUDGE: You will not burn?

TING: Not until you hear —

JUDGE: Then you will suffocate. Lock him in an oven with no air. *(The GUARDS grab TING.)* **Not now. In the morning. Haven't you been paying attention?** *(The GUARDS, MOMMA XING, and the BOYS enter.)*

MOMMA XING: Still nothing?

TING: Nope.

MOMMA XING: Group hug. *(They ALL hug and ZING is left in PING's place.)*

NARRATOR 3: The next morning, Zing was brought to the village oven. *(Which can be a refrigerator box painted with bricks and stuff. The CROWD is there again and cheer as the GUARDS bring in ZING.)*

JUDGE: Ding, I order you to be placed in this air tight oven. *(GUARDS place ZING in the oven.)*

NARRATOR 3: But this time, the judge wasn't taking any chances. He waited a whole day. *(NARRATOR 2 walks by with a cardboard cut out of a sun.)* **And the entire night.** *(NARRATOR 1 walks by with cardboard cut out of a moon.)* **And finally, the next day, he opened the oven door.**

ZING: *(Popping out.)* **That was a good sleep. Who's up for some flapjacks?** *(The CROWD gasps.)*

JUDGE: How can this be? We have tried to eliminate you in every possible way. It must be that you are innocent.

ZING: That is for the people to decide, my lord. If only you will hear my side of the story.

NARRATOR 1: And so the judge finally did listen to Ding's side of the story. And the entire crowd listened, too. *(DING is miming how he waved and waved.)*

JUDGE: You warned them!

DING: Several times.

JUDGE: *(Turning on MACKEREL and SQUID)* **You two lied to me.**

MACKEREL and SQUID: Uh-oh. Gotta blast. *(And THEY take off running.)*

NARRATOR 2: And so Mackerel and Squid ran away. And Ding was set free.

JUDGE: I am so sorry, Ding. You are free to go.

NARRATOR 2: The judge retired.

JUDGE: If I can no longer hear all sides of a story, what is there to judge? *(Hands his scepter to a guard.)*

NARRATOR 2: And Momma Xing and her sons all lived …

EVERYONE: Happily ever after.

TOMMY: *(To the S group)* Sorry, we thought you were done with the ball.

SUSIE: Guess we shoulda told ya.

TABBY: We didn't know.

SAMMY: Our fault really.

TERRY: Hey, want to play some dodge ball?

S GROUP: Yeah. *(The groups run Off-stage leaving just the NARRATORS On-stage.)*

NARRATOR 3: Perhaps if we all just open our ears we can all live —

NARRATORS: Happily ever after.

It's a Wrap

OK, so all that you've just done is "behind the scenes." In kid vernacular, this was your homework; you chose your play.

It's time to make copies of the show you've chosen, one for every actor in the show, and then make about five extra just in case. You can usually save money on this by e-mailing it out to everyone in your cast, and they can each print their own copy.

At your next rehearsal, you will need:

• The copies of the show

• Plain white labels that the kids can turn into name badges

• Fun colored pens

• Pencils

• A theatre game or two

• Your sense of humor

Trivia Time

* **The Bard is Shakespeare's nickname. Calling a dude "The Bard" is like calling him "The Poet" and is a testament to his monumental status among the great writers in English.**

** **The fairy tale character who spun straw into gold was … come on, you can guess it. Drum roll … Rumpelstiltskin. Good for you. Now, can you name all seven dwarfs? In five seconds? *Go!***

Chapter Three

Writing Your Own Play

"What if the story was to take place in a ninja village with floating toilets?"

Warning — What we're about to embark upon may be dangerous. You may discover things about yourself you didn't know. So if you are faint of heart, if your sense of adventure is going to bed without flossing, then heed my warning: skip the next two chapters!

But if you long for excitement, fear no boundaries, still believe in magic, or the Tooth Fairy, read on, **MacDuff***.

You're about to enter a world where the only limitation is your imagination. You're going to write a play with the kids. Technically, you're actually doing an adaptation. But by the time you're done, it will be so unique that it will truly be original.

And it's so easy. Don't tell my other writer friends I said this, but most stories can be broken down into a very basic formula. Apply this "formula" to any story and you will see how simple it is to craft a play.

Who knows, you may even become a published playwright.

Once Upon a Time in Cindyland ...

When I was directing the play *Steppin' Out* at a little community theatre in Sherman Oaks, the publishing house pulled the rights, which means they denied us the ability to do the show. We never did find out why. Anyhoo, here we were with a theatre — a miraculous thing in L.A., — a cast and no show. Well, my husband, being my husband, wasn't going to let opportunity knock and not answer the door. He wrote his own. In less than a week, mind you. A western called *Wild Dust*. We went back into rehearsals and mounted the show. We didn't invite anyone because we figured, "a play written in a week, how good could it be?" As it turns out, a reviewer from *Variety* magazine — one of the more important Hollywood mags — came out and saw the show. She wrote an incredible review. Samuel French read the review and called us. They wanted to know why they hadn't been invited to come see the show. "Um," we said. (Hey, we're writers, not public speakers.) They asked if they could publish it. Since then, *Wild Dust* has been performed by theatres all across the country. We've had close to ten shows published. And you can, too!

Cindy's Basic Elements of Play Structure

"Let's start at the very beginning, a very good place to start." * *

Please note here that I said, *Cindy's* basic elements. I do not claim to be an authority on writing plays. Certainly, there are many more teachers out there who could offer you the whys and wherefores. Type in playwriting at Amazon.com and you'll get over five thousand hits. So there's lots of advice out there to be had.

I'm going to break down a story into seven very basic components. It's actually a bit shameful how simple I'm making this. But hey, we're busy parents and teachers and we want to write something for our kids in the least amount of time. And we want to build our confidence as writers, too.

Cindy's View of the World #458B+2

Writing begets writing, so the more you do, the braver you get. The more risks you take, the better your writing becomes.

Once Upon a Time in Cindyland ...

While we were on staff at Disney they decided to do *Pirates of the Caribbean* as an animated film — this was three years before the Johnny Depp movie came out. We were lucky enough to be chosen as writers. We wrote a script that we were way proud of! Sadly, it was abandoned for the live action script that eventually got made. Ah, the life of a writer. But at the final tally, we had done over sixty-seven drafts of the script; each rewrite was a little better than the last.

Oh, don't worry, there aren't sixty-seven drafts in your future, just one fantastic play ... then maybe another. Then another? Keep writing!

Hero

The first of the seven components is, of course, the hero. This is our "good guy." The dude or dudette who has a story to tell and we're telling it. Most times we prefer this person to be likable. For example, if someone were writing a play about a dedicated parent or teacher, you, dear reader, would be the hero.

Hero's Goal

What good is a hero if they don't have a worthy goal? Something we can root for. Back to our example, your very worthy goal is to mount a production with a herd of little people.

Villain

This is our "bad guy." He doesn't want us to accomplish our worthy goal. The villain doesn't have to be a he — the villain can be a she or an animal or something environmental, like a storm or an asteroid. He or she can be a *they*. Like a committee of well-intentioned people, or an evil, faceless corporation.

Obstacles

This is the basis of all drama. What stands in the way of our hero obtaining his or her goal? The villain wants to stop the hero, because the villain has his or her own agenda. And both must be willing to stop at nothing to achieve their goal.

So let's say you, our hero, want to put on a show with the kids. Your villain might be a parent who sees what you're doing as destructive. This parent wants to stop you. They may sabotage rehearsals, undermine your authority, and refuse time or resources. These are all obstacles to keep you from your goal.

Setting

Where does our story take place? Is it under the sea, on a mountain top, or in a MPR?

Time

What year does our magical tale take place? With you, my dear hero, the time would be today.

Outcome

OK, maybe it's because I worked at Disney for so many years, but I've got to say, I prefer *Happily Ever After* to those ambivalent endings like *The Lady and the Tiger*. I know that's simplistic. I know it's tried and true. But we're talking about little people here and it's important that we send positive messages. So my advice is to have the hero learn something. And have him or her get his or her heart's desire.

Once Upon a Time in Cindyland ...

When we were doing *Beauty and the Beast: The Enchanted Christmas*, our director could not get behind the fact that the story was so linear. He wanted to tell it in a *non-linear way* — translation: the story should be out of order, lots of arty cutaways and memory cutbacks. The thing is, this was a Disney film. Disney, at that point, didn't do non-linear animated filmmaking. So we had lots of fun rewriting a script that was liked by everyone, right up to Michael Eisner, because the director had this "vision." Aaaach!

Cindy's View of the World #968Q @

My advice, stick to the tried and true, especially when you're writing your first piece.

Pick a Story

*Jack and the Beanstalk****

Let's start with the basic story that we all know.

Once upon a time there was this little dude named Jack who lived with his mom in a shack because they were incredibly poor. But they did have a cow. I'll call her Bessie. Jack's mom asked Jack to take Bessie to town where he could sell her. Jack did as he was told, for he was a pretty good kid, but along the way he met a salesman. The guy said he would give Jack three magical beans for the cow. Jack thought this was an awesome idea and went home with his beans. His mom was really cheesed at him and threw the beans outside. Jack went to bed and, while he slept, the beans grew into a giant beanstalk. Jack, probably not wanting to face his mom in the morning, climbed the beanstalk. There he found a castle inhabited by a mean old giant who was really rich and had a goose that could lay a golden egg. Jack stole the goose and was chased by the giant to the beanstalk. Jack shimmied down the stalk, with the giant on his tail. When Jack got to the bottom, he cut the stalk down. The giant fell to the earth. Jack was left with a money-making goose. They all lived happily ever after.

So that's the basic tale. Let's break it down into our seven story elements.

Who is our hero in this story? Jack

What does he want? To feed his hungry family.

Who is the villain? The giant

What are the obstacles? The unknown fear of where the beanstalk leads. The giant's size and power. Jack is far from home. The goose is hard to get.

What's the setting? A castle in the clouds

When does the story take place? That's kind of vague. Let's call it no time.

What's the outcome? Jack gets the goose and he and his mom live happily ever after.

OK, so that's pretty easy to follow, I hope.

Adapting the Story

This is where it gets fun. Let's take each element and see how we can recreate it. We'll start with the setting and the time, because once you create these, the others will flow from these choices.

Does the setting have to be a castle in the clouds? Nope. It can be any location we want: under the sea, the Serengeti, a village in Peru, or an urban city street.

The time can be present day, two hundred years ago, five thousand years into the future. It can be a specific time, like Halloween or Christmas Eve.

Who says Jack, the hero, has to be a boy? He can be a ninja warrior or a Knight of Old. He can even be a girl. An Amazon Princess or a shy third grader. Heck, who says the hero has to be human? He can be a dog, a narwhal, or a unicorn. However, if you've already decided the story takes place in the Wild West, then odds are, Jack is *not* going to be a mermaid.

What does the hero want? Jack wanted to feed his hungry family, but what's to keep him from broadening that goal? Maybe Jack wants to become a famous musician/singer, find a hidden treasure, or to return the universe to the rightful heirs.

Who is the villain? The villain can be: a land baron, a Nazi general, a thief, or a desperate housewife.

What are the obstacles? Now this depends on whom we chose for our villain and our hero. Let's say our hero is a cowboy, then probably we'd want to make our villain the land baron. And the hero wants to settle the land and build a home for his family. But the evil land baron wants that land free for his cattle. Ah ha, conflict and obstacles. How will the villain stop our hero?

He'll talk to him, he'll vandalize the buildings, he'll rally an army of cowboys, or start a stampede. However, I do think our play could be quite fun if our hero was the cowboy but our villain turned out to be the whale. But that gets a little whacky and you have to have a strong stomach for that. Kudos to you if you do.

The outcome? The hero gets his or her heart's desire. Again, it depends on who our hero is and what they want. If the hero were a mermaid under the sea, she probably gets the legs. If she were from a distant galaxy far, far away, she saves the universe.

OK, so now we have the pieces and we've seen how they can change. Let's try all of this in the classroom.

Taking it to the Streets

You will need:

- Enough copies for everyone of the story you've chosen to adapt.
- Your list of the seven elements, which you could put on index cards to remind you what they are.
- Plain white labels that will become nametags
- Colorful markers
- Pencils and paper
- A chalkboard or dry erase board and chalk or dry erase pens
- Your sense of humor

Step One — Decorate the Labels

Just like we tired parents and teachers need our downtime when we come home from work, little people need their transition time into the wonderful world of creating. These labels will totally do the trick. Give each child a label and a plethora of pretty pens and tell them to write their names. But let them have fun with it; they can write their name in cursive, block letters, or Ancient Sanskrit — whatever their imaginations will allow. Let them draw pictures or bubbles or ice cream cones next to their name. The point is to loosen up the creative muscle and have fun. Do this craft each week — while you're in the writing process. But don't be limited by just labels, if you want to do name cards, picture frame shapes, or tattoos, that's up to you.

Step Two — Read the Story

You're going to read the story *and* play theatre games to break up the monotony for the children, and to keep opening up their creativity — and yours. Also, don't just read and play games. Discuss the story as you go. Ask them questions about it: what do you think of the Princess? Would you rather be the dragon or the boy? Who here has ever seen a big red dog?

Don't be afraid to ask them what they liked and didn't like. Let them share their thoughts and feelings with you. Opinions are a wonderful thing. They help the kids formulate their own ideas and their own passions. You also get to learn a bit about yourself as well. What do you like? What didn't you like?

Step Three — Break Down the Story

This step happens only when the story has been completely read and discussed, not one minute before. Now ask the kids, as a group, to break down the story with you. Start by asking: Who is the hero? Who is the villain? And as they're answering you, write it down on the chalkboard, just as I did for you a few pages ago.

Example:

Hero — Jack

Villain — The giant

Step Four — Create a New Story

Now that you've broken down the story into the seven elements, let's rebuild it with their ideas. *Every* idea is a good one, so write it down.

Ask them for: other hero ideas, other villain ideas, other setting ideas, and other time ideas. They may get a little confused about obstacles, but they may not. Write it *all* down. What's neat here is that they'll tell you stories as they talk to you. This comes in incredibly handy, as you'll see when you read the scripts at the end of the next chapter.

Step Five – Vote

There's a plethora of great ideas on the chalkboard, but writing is about making choices. So it's time to vote. By show of hands, ask the kids what their favorites are. Start with the hero. Take the top three. Keep going right on down the line until they've voted on everything. Erase anything that didn't make the cut.

Step Six – Have them Write *Their* Story Down

Hand out those papers and pencils and have them write down their own story with the element ideas you've left on the board. Some may end up just drawing pictures. Some may write only a word or two. Some may give you epic tales — thank goodness for those children. Don't have this go on for more than a half hour. The kids have been in school all day. They don't want to spend their fun time writing. At least most won't. You be the judge. If they're saying, "Oh please, five more minutes," then for heaven's sake give them five more minutes. Then, collect their stories.

Step Seven — Wave Bye-Bye

Take a moment as you exit the classroom to notice what you've just done for a passel of children. You turned reading and writing into something magical. And just wait until they read their play.

Cindy's TLC Tip #11

"We here at the Parent Volunteer Institute would like to award you, oh heroic mommy or daddy or teacher, the You Rock Award." Now write your acceptance speech. You can deliver it to your shower wall, your empty car, or your family if you're really brave. And what the heck, buy your self a little gold statue. You deserve it.

Trivia Time

*MacDuff was the villain in MacBeth. OK, this has nothing to do with anything, but there's a term we use in storytelling called *McGuffin*. It's the thing that drives the plot forward. In a caper story, it would be the heist. (You probably didn't care about that did you?)

**From the song "Do-Re-Mi" in *The Sound of Music.*

***Funny how fate can play a hand in our lives. After Flip and I finished doing *Jackie and the Beanstalk* for a group of grade school kids, we commented how fun it would be to write it as a movie. Well lo and behold, an independent production company, Avalon, contacted us not long after and asked us to write a low budget movie for them. "Which one?" we asked. "Jack and the Beanstalk." And no, they didn't know we had done this little play for a group of kids. Oh, by the way, the movie should be coming out sometime in the near future. Please go see it.

 **Chapter Four**

Rewriting the Show

"Quiet, I'm writing."

"Taking a new step, uttering a new word is what people fear most."

— Dostoyevsky

It's time to roll up our sleeves and start writing — right after I dust off my armoire. OK, that's done. We're going to hit the keyboard and tell our tale ... as soon as I make lunch.

Do you know why writers have the cleanest houses? Because they will do anything to avoid writing a page, anything! For example, they might decide to repaint the inside of the garage. Or they might regale you with tales of their youth: when Flip and I started writing *Lion King II*, we had ten days to turn over our first draft. Ten days?! We literally slept in shifts. Flip had written a sequence and I didn't have the time I normally have to study it, ponder it, think about the subtle nuances Flip might have been exploring. So I found a shortcut, which was far more effective, I woke him up in the middle of the night by whacking him in the head. "Why did you change this?" I croaked (cut me some slack, it was like four in the morning). Funny, that script took us the least amount of time, but it's the one we're most proud of. Although, to this day, I would have liked Kiara to have been more empowered. She was cut down a lot from our original draft.

I guess it's time to write, huh?

Cindy's TLC Tip #007

You are Bond, James Bond, 'cause only a hero of Bondic proportions could survive a few weeks with the little villains. Oops, I mean children. In celebration, I want you to watch any Bond film. I personally recommend Daniel Craig's who did *Casino Royale*. Oh, I know there are those out there who will live and die by Connery, but really, Craig was so much better. So grab your drink of choice, place it in a martini glass, kick up your feet and watch the double-O. Now, here's my favorite part, when the movie is over, head to your closest mirror — you probably want to do this in the bathroom with the door shut and everyone in your house asleep — stare at your reflection and say "I'm Bond. (Insert your name here) Bond." Wink. Are you awesome or what?

Cindy's TLC Tip #007 continued

What, watching girls with great bodies prance around in skimpy outfits isn't your thing? Girlfriend, it's time to rent *The Devil Wears Prada*. Pretend to wear each and every outfit — when she starts to look really hot — and then marvel at the ending, 'cause what girl in their right mind would do that? (I can't tell you! That will ruin the movie.) But believe me, her last gesture is a totally big buy.

Adapting the Story

To simplify this and make it as easy for you as possible, I'm going to walk you through how we turned *Jack and the Beanstalk* into *Jackie and the Beanstalk*.

What you will need:

• The stories the kids wrote

• A vat of coffee or anything caffeinated

• A block of time

• Belief in yourself

Step One – Tell the Story

Start with telling the story. Don't worry about getting all the subtle nuances of the story, just tell it as you remember it.

Step Two – Changing Your Story

I always find it easiest to understand how to do something if I see how someone else did it.

Once Upon a Time in Cindyland ...

When we started this project, we had many more girls than boys, which happens a lot. Since we knew from our theatre games which of the kids were the most outgoing, we had a pretty good idea who our main characters were going to be. So we simply started breaking down the story. We started with the setting.

Armed with our chalkboard, we asked the kids to give us alternate settings besides a fairytale world. They shouted up their responses and we marked 'em all down. Old England. Hawaii. On the moon. On a speck of dust. Inside Billy's booger nose. (You may get a lot of these.) But we wrote them all down. Then we moved on to the time.

Once Upon a Time in Cindyland ... continued

We got the wild West. The robotic future. Ten minutes from now. July 11, 2004. (We're still pondering that one.) Again, we wrote them all down. Now, being a mom with a little foresight and no idea how much help, if any, I was going to have on this little journey, I deftly directed the kids to a setting of an inner city, and the time of right now. See, this way, I knew we wouldn't have to sew twenty-five knights and damsels costumes. Modern day street clothes would work great for costumes. Thinking ahead, all the time.

So now that we had our time and place, we looked at the hero. Again, we wrote down each and every suggestion. Well, we knew the hero couldn't be a dragon or a robot because they don't exist in an inner city today. And since we had a sense of who our strongest actors would be, we ended up making Jack a girl. A normal, modern day girl named Jackie.

Being a writer, it was exciting to see kids getting excited about writing.

Next we looked at some other elements we could change. The cow. Since a modern city girl probably wouldn't have a cow, what else could she have that was the most valuable thing in the world? Pretty much every kid agreed it would be a kickin' MP3 player. So the cow now became an MP3.

When we talked about what we could substitute for the beanstalk we got suggestions of ladders, jet packs, trampolines, and stairs. But when the idea of an escalator came up, it opened another line of thought. Why did the stairs have to go up? Maybe they could go down. And so the giant's city above the clouds became an abandoned subway station.

Looking to find an alternative for the villain, we knew our little cadre of elementary school kids didn't have a giant of any kind. Four-foot-six was the tallest of the tall. So we decided to make the giant a figurative giant in the music industry.

What follows is the play we wrote. First read and enjoy it. But after that, analyze it, use it as your template if you get lost, borrow from it if you need a character. It is my gift to you.

Jackie and the Beanstalk

By Flip Kobler and Cindy Marcus (that's me!)

(The Storyteller, or DREAMWEAVER as we're gonna call 'em, walks in front of the curtain, wearing a Lakers jersey and dribbling a basketball. The DREAMWEAVER stops and looks to the audience.)

DREAMWEAVER: Yo. They say there are a million stories in the city. A million. So how come the ones we're told all start with "Once Upon A Time"? What's up with that? But tonight we got a whole new deal. Actually, we got an old old story, but this one happens Once Upon Today. *(Music sneaks up, all urban and cool. Sounds of the city drift over us.)*

DREAMWEAVER: It started in a city, like any city. *(The curtains open and we see the city bustling with activity. A few girls jump rope. FAST TOMMY is doing three-card Monte. Coupla guys are playing basketball, which the DREAMWEAVER joins for a moment. Someone plays a Game Boy. DOOMCRYER walks through the mob, wearing a sandwich board. One side says "The End is Coming.")*

DOOMCRYER: The end is coming! The end is coming! *(DOOMCRYER turns and we see the other side of the board. "No Intermission." A young reporter, MAY WEATHERS, takes the stage, her cameraman, QUINCY, filming the action. A clapboard operator, CLAPPER, is always interjecting himself or herself into the camera, marking the scenes. MAY positions herself for best pose.)*

MAY WEATHERS: This is May Weathers for Kidsnews dot com.

CLAPPER: Kidsnews dot com. Marker. *(Clap)*

QUINCY THE CAMERAMAN: What are you doing?

CLAPPER: Marking the scene.

QUINCY THE CAMERAMAN: Dude.

MAY WEATHERS: I'm here downtown where there have been reports of a cow running wild in the streets.

CLAPPER: Cue the cow! *(A cow enters. Actually, it's just two kids. The front of the cow wears horns on his or her head and a long cow print poncho. Another kid is hunched under the backside of the poncho, making up the rear end. The front half is totally cheesed off all the time. The back half is perky.)*

COW FRONT: Moo. Moo. Man, I can't believe I'm doin' this. How embarrassing. Moo.

MAY WEATHERS: Excuse me, Mister Cow. May Weathers with Kidsnews dot com. Can you tell us why you're running amok?

COW FRONT: Amok? What's that mean? You can't talk normal? Geez.

MAY WEATHERS: Can you tell us why you're running wild?

COW FRONT: Do I look like I'm running? Are you blind? Geez.

COW BACK: Don't mind him. He's just Mister Crabby-Pants. Aren't ya?

COW FRONT: Quit it.

COW BACK: Aren't ya?

COW FRONT: Quit it.

MAY WEATHERS: Can you tell us what you're doing in the city?

COW FRONT: I don't know. We're a hold-over from the old story. Jack. Beanstalk. Cow. It's like a forced cameo. I should be relaxing on a farm.

COW BACK: I like it here. We can get nachos.

MAY WEATHERS: *(The COW wanders off and MAY turns to the camera.)* There you have it. Panic in the streets. I'm May Weathers for Kidsnews dot com.

CLAPPER: Kidsnews dot com. Marker. *(Clap)*

QUINCY THE CAMERAMAN: Dude.

MAY WEATHERS: *(To the Cameraman)* How was that?

QUINCY THE CAMERAMAN: Perfect. You're gold, baby, gold. You're the dot com queen.

MAY WEATHERS: I know. *(She and QUINCY wander off.)*

DREAMWEAVER: But our story isn't about cows or the city. It's really about one girl. One very special girl. *(Now ALICE from* Alice in Wonderland *comes running on.)*

ALICE: Oh me. Oh my. Oh dear.

DREAMWEAVER: What are you doing here?

ALICE: I seem to have lost my way. Have you seen a white rabbit? 'Bout this tall?

RABBIT: *(Entering)* I'm late. I'm late. For a very important date. Whoa —

DREAMWEAVER: You're in the wrong story.

ALICE: Oh my.

RABBIT: Are you sure?

DREAMWEAVER: Yeah. I think you're supposed to be over at Fair Oaks tonight.

ALICE: Fair Oaks. Are you sure? *(DREAMWEAVER nods.)* Oh my.

RABBIT: That's across town. Can your mom give us a ride?

ALICE: I don't think so.

RABBIT: Oh man, we're late. We're late. *(THEY go running off. DREAMWEAVER turns to the audience.)*

DREAMWEAVER: Sorry about that. Our story is about a *different* girl. A great girl. Jackie.

CLAPPER: *(Running on.)* Cue Jackie. *(Running off. JACKIE enters wearing headphones and boppin' to her MP3 player. She boogies to a tune only she can hear.)*

DREAMWEAVER: Jackie's pretty cool. But she got some big dreams, dude. 'Cause Jackie loves music. *(Just then three girls run up, TRISH, TINA, and TYLER, who are never apart. They're like on a permanent sugar rush and tend to scream like groupies. THEY rush to JACKIE and squeal.)*

TRISH: Jackie! Jackie.

JACKIE: Hey, guys.

GIRLS: *(Scream)* Ahhhh!

TINA: Did you hear? Switchfoot is playing the Roxie.

TYLER: The Roxie!

TRISH and TINA: *Ahhhh!*

TYLER: *Ahhhh!*

JACKIE: No way!

TRISH: Total way!

TYLER: Total.

TRISH: Switchfoot! *Ahhhh!*

TYLER: *Ahhhh!*

JACKIE: Oh man.

TINA: Wanna go?

JACKIE: Duh. Yeah.

TYLER: Yeah.

TRISH: *Ahhhh!* This is great. Tickets are fifty bucks.

JACKIE: What? Oh man. You know what, I can't go.

TINA: Why not?

TRISH: 'Cause she doesn't have the money, doof.

TYLER: Yeah, doof.

TINA: Why don't you ask your uncle for it?

JACKIE: Fifty bucks is a lot of money. He doesn't have it.

TRISH: Maybe if he got a job.

TINA: *(Whacking TRISH)* **Shhhh.** *(TRISH whacks TINA back.)*

JACKIE: He had to hock his guitar to pay rent.

TINA: You could sell your MP3 on Ebay.

JACKIE: Like that's gonna happen. I'd rather sell my left foot and half my fingers. This is my music. I'm going to be the greatest songwriter in the world some day.

TRISH: Whatever.

TRISH and TINA: Switchfoot. *Ahhhh!*

TYLER: *Ahhhh! (THEY run off, leaving JACKIE to look lost and miserable. The DOOMCRYER enters with another sandwich board. "My Stomach is Rumbling" on one side.)*

DOOMCRYER: My stomach is rumbling. My stomach is rumbling.

JACKIE: *(Handing him a bag of chips)* It's all I got.

DOOMCRYER: The end of hunger is near. The end of hunger is near. *(Turns to reveal the other side of the board. "Thank You.")*

DREAMWEAVER: Jackie lived in a third floor walkup with her brother and her Uncle Vinnie. *(Two stagehands move sets and props and basically do all the cool stage handy stuff. They change the scene to inside the house. One stagehand is there holding up a Styrofoam door. JACKIE fumbles for her keys and mimes opening the lock. The door opens as the stagehand makes a squeaky hinge noise. JACKIE's brother LITTLE STEVIE is there.)*

LITTLE STEVIE: Jackie, you're late. How come you're late, huh? Will you help me with my homework? Huh? Will you? Huh?

JACKIE: Sure. Where's Uncle Vinnie?

UNCLE VINNIE: Right here.

JACKIE: *(Looking him over)* **Who are you?**

UNCLE VINNIE: Uncle Vinnie.

JACKIE: You're not my Uncle Vinnie.

UNCLE VINNIE: Yes, I am.

JACKIE: You can't be, you're a kid.

UNCLE VINNIE: Noh-uh.

JACKIE: What are you, like eleven?

UNCLE VINNIE: I'm thirty-four.

JACKIE: No way. I have you in homeroom.

UNCLE VINNIE: In this story, I'm your Uncle Vinnie.

JACKIE: That's stupid. We can't get an adult to play the uncle? He's a kid.

UNCLE VINNIE: Am not.

JACKIE: Are too. *(THEY argue that back and forth. It gets louder and louder. The DOOMCRYER enters with a new sign, "The Scene's in Trouble.")*

DOOMCRYER: The scene's in trouble. The scene's in trouble.

TYLER: Scene's in trouble.

TRISH and TINA: Switchfoot. *Ahhhh!*

TYLER: *Ahhhh! (The stage is full of kids running around screaming like it's the end of the world, including primary kids. A REFEREE comes on.)*

REFEREE: Break it up. Break it up. *(When the stage is clear, the REFEREE turns to the audience.)* Delay of story. Five yard penalty against Jackie. Scene continues. *(Runs off.)*

JACKIE: I'm sorry, "Uncle Vinnie."

UNCLE VINNIE: That's OK, sweetheart.

LITTLE STEVIE: What's for dinner, huh? What? Huh?

UNCLE VINNIE: Yeah, here's the thing. My unemployment ran out last week. We're tapped out, kids. We don't have any money and I don't have anything left to sell. I'm sorry.

JACKIE: It's OK.

UNCLE VINNIE: No, it's not. I let you guys down.

LITTLE STEVIE: Are we gonna starve? Huh? Are we? Starve and dehydrate and die?

JACKIE: We'll be OK.

LITTLE STEVIE: How? Huh? How?

UNCLE VINNIE: I'll think of something. *(VINNIE drapes an arm around LITTLE STEVIE and walks him Off-stage. JACKIE looks at her MP3 a long time, making a choice. Then she walks off through the door, the stagehand making the squeaky hinge noise again. She exits Off-stage as the lights come up on the DREAMWEAVER standing outside. The stagehands change the scene back to the street.)*

DREAMWEAVER: Jackie wasn't exactly brain dead. She knew what she had to do.

CLAPPER: (*Running on*) **Cue the table!** (*Running off. FAST TOMMY comes on with his three-card Monte table, which is just a stagehand kneeling, holding a cardboard tabletop over his or her head.*)

FAST TOMMY: **Round and round she goes, where she stops, nobody knows. Keep your eye on the cards, find the ace of hearts.** (*Seeing JACKIE*) **Hey, 'sup?**

JACKIE: **Hi.**

FAST TOMMY: **Wanna play? Five bucks. Guess it right and I'll give you ten.**

JACKIE: **And if I guess wrong?**

FAST TOMMY: **I keep the five.**

JACKIE: **I don't have any money.**

FAST TOMMY: **Bummer. Gather round guys, round and round she goes!**

JACKIE: **Wanna play for this?** (*She puts her MP3 on the table. FAST TOMMY looks at it.*)

FAST TOMMY: **What's the sitch?**

JACKIE: **That's my MP3. You could get a lot for that on eBay.**

FAST TOMMY: **Why don't you eBay it?**

JACKIE: **Don't have the time. I need the money now.**

FAST TOMMY: **I'll give ya twenty bucks.**

JACKIE: **Twenty?! That's it? Come on, that's everything I've got.**

FAST TOMMY: **Man, I've been offered a lot but never everything.**

JACKIE: **All my hopes and dreams are in that thing. A hundred dollars?**

FAST TOMMY: **Tell ya what ...** (*Pulls JACKIE aside.*) **You can't put a price on your dreams. But I'll tell ya what I will give you.** (*He looks around to be sure they're alone and pulls out a handful of computer chips.*)

JACKIE: **Computer chips?**

FAST TOMMY: **Shhhh! You want everyone to hear? These aren't just computer chips. These are magic computer chips.**

JACKIE: **Magic. Dude, you're crazy.**

FAST TOMMY: **Wait.**

JACKIE: **You're whacked. Your brain is off the radar.**

FAST TOMMY: **OK, not magic. But just as good. This is nanite technology. Tiny little robots in these chips can make anything.**

JACKIE: **I've heard of nanites.**

FAST TOMMY: **Sure, smart techno chick like you. Plug these chips into any computer and they will make all your dreams come true.**

JACKIE: **Really?**

FAST TOMMY: **If I'm lyin' I'm dyin'.**

JACKIE: **Deal.** (*JACKIE leaves the MP3, takes the chips, and runs Off-stage. She passes DREAMWEAVER as he or she enters. Behind the DREAMWEAVER the scene is changing back into the apartment. Door stagehand is there again.*)

DREAMWEAVER: So Jackie took the nanite chips and went running home. Uncle Vinnie wasn't happy.

UNCLE VINNIE: You did what?

JACKIE: These are magic chips. They can make our dreams come true.

UNCLE VINNIE: There's no such thing as magic.

LITTLE STEVIE: No way. For real? In real life?

JACKIE: Not really magic. It's nanite technology. Tiny little robots —

UNCLE VINNIE: There's no such thing as nanites. They just made that up for Star Trek.

LITTLE STEVIE: Next Gen or Deep Space Nine?

JACKIE: No. You'll see. We put these in a computer —

UNCLE VINNIE: We don't own a computer.

JACKIE: But the library has one. Maybe we could use theirs.

UNCLE VINNIE: Jackie. He scammed you. These are worthless. *(He throws the chips out the window. Jackie looks disappointed. They head Off-stage as the DREAMWEAVER steps forward and the set changes to the city again.)*

DREAMWEAVER: So Jackie gave up the thing that meant the most to her. And for a big fat nothing. Or so she thought. *(The DOOMCRYER lays down and goes to sleep.)* **Because while the city slept, those nanites went to work.**

CLAPPER: *(Running on and whispering)* **Cue the nanites.** *(Exits. Lights go down. The primary play kids come out in the dark with flashlights. They shine the lights at the audience, looking like pixie fairies. The lights dance and play as the music plays. Finally, they vanish Off-stage and the lights come back on. There is a handrail to an escalator and a sign pointing down to the subway that read, "Hopes & Dreams Station.")*

DREAMWEAVER: **When Jackie left for school the next day —**

JACKIE: *(Entering and seeing the subway)* **Whoa!**

DREAMWEAVER: **— she knew the nanites had been real.**

JACKIE: Cool.

DREAMWEAVER: **She just had to follow her hopes and dreams.** *(JACKIE stands behind the railing flat and pretends to go down. The stagehands are moving scenery behind them to make it look like they're going deep into the earth.)*

DREAMWEAVER: **So Jackie went down. And down. And down. But, she wasn't alone.**

LITTLE STEVIE: Hey, Jackie, wait up, huh? Can ya? Huh? *(Joins her on the escalator.)*

JACKIE: What are you doing here?

LITTLE STEVIE: I'm coming with you.

JACKIE: No way.

LITTLE STEVIE: Yeah. Everybody wants to see where this goes.

JACKIE: What do you mean *everybody*?

CLAPPER: *(Runs on.)* **Cue, everybody.** *(Exits. The COW, MAY, QUINCY,* *and DREAMWEAVER join them on the escalator.)*

COW FRONT: Moo. Moo. This is just stupid. How is a cow supposed to ride an escalator? What does a cow want in a subway? I mean, geez.

COW BACK: Oh lighten up, Mister Crabby-Pants.

COW FRONT: Quit it.

COW BACK: Crabby-Pants.

COW FRONT: Quit it.

MAY WEATHERS: I'm May Weathers for Kidsnews dot com. I'm going deep into the bowels of the earth —

QUINCY THE CAMERAMAN: Wait. Can you say bowels on line?

MAY WEATHERS: I think so, should we do another take?

JACKIE: Wait. Stop. You shouldn't be here. *(She looks to the DREAMWEAVER.)* This is wrong. I'm supposed to do this alone.

DREAMWEAVER: *(As he exits)* Just go with it.

JACKIE: Fine. This can't get much worse.

DOOMCRYER: The end is near! The end is near! Watch your step! *(They ALL get off the escalator. The stagehands make it vanish and turn the scene to the subway station.)*

JACKIE: Where are we?

QUINCY THE CAMERAMAN: In a hole, baby. Deep in some hole.

RABBIT: *(Running on with ALICE)* We're late. We're late. And we're lost.

JACKIE: Not again.

MAY WEATHERS: Can you tell us what you're doing here?

ALICE: Oh dear. We fell down the wrong hole.

COW FRONT: OK, this is just stupid. *(Others join in, ad-libbing. It turns into a fight until the REFEREE comes in.)*

REFEREE: Time out. Time. *(Breaks up the fight, and turns to the audience.)* After reviewing the script, we find unnecessary confusion on Alice and the Rabbit. Technical foul. You're out of here. Still first act. *(Wrangles ALICE and the RABBIT Off-stage. When it's finally quiet —)*

JACKIE: Where are we? Hello? *(A voice Off-stage mimics her echo.)* Anyone there?

ECHO VOICE: Anyone there?

JACKIE: Echo!

ECHO VOICE: Stop shouting. You'll scare the bats.

LITTLE STEVIE: Bats?!

ECHO VOICE: *Bats?!* *(The primary play kids rush across stage holding up little bats on sticks. They run around screeching like bats as the music does batty stuff. ALL duck and cover until the bats vanish Off-stage. When it settles —)*

MAY WEATHERS: Did you get that?

QUINCY THE CAMERAMAN: Gold, baby. Pure gold.

LITTLE STEVIE: Jackie, where are we? Huh? Where? Huh?

JACKIE: I don't know.

MAY WEATHERS: We seem to be in an abandoned subway station.

COW FRONT: Moo.

JACKIE: Look at the sign. "Hopes & Dreams Station." This must be the place where your hopes and dreams come true.

LITTLE STEVIE: That's cool. Huh? Cool?

COW FRONT: Hopes and dreams? Have you smelled this place? It stinks.

COW BACK: That was me. Sorry.

COW FRONT: I'm a cow in a subway station. I mean, geez. This is not my dream place, OK.

LITTLE STEVIE: So how's it work? Huh? How?

JACKIE: I don't know.

COW FRONT: Well duh. She doesn't know. What a surprise.

COW BACK: Oh be nice.

COW FRONT: I am nice!

COW BACK: I don't think so.

COW FRONT: You're not supposed to think. You're the butt, I'm the head.

COW BACK: Right now you're acting like both. (*Two janitors enter, PETE and REPETE, with brooms and mops.*)

REPETE: How come I hafta mop? I always mop. Why don't you mop?

PETE: 'Cause that's not my job.

REPETE: Why is it my job?

PETE: Did you make the mess? No. I had to. You want me to make the mess *and* clean it up?

REPETE: Well …

PETE: Fine. I just didn't think you were that selfish.

REPETE: OK, wait. I'm sorry.

JACKIE: Excuse me —

PETE: *Ahhhh!*

REPETE: *Ahhhh!*

JACKIE: *Ahhhh!*

PETE, REPETE, and JACKIE: *Ahhhh!*

EVERYONE: *Ahhhh!*

COW FRONT: Mooooo.

JACKIE: Easy. We're not going to hurt you.

REPETE: Who are you?

JACKIE: I'm Jackie.

PETE: Where'd you come from? How'd you get here?

JACKIE: We just took the escalator — Hey! Where's the escalator? (*They ALL run around frantically.*) It was just here. Where'd it go?

REPETE: It's gone.

JACKIE: What do you mean, gone?

PETE: It's vanished, man. That's the way it always is.

JACKIE: What do you mean, always? How do we get out of here?

REPETE: You don't. There's no way out.

MAY WEATHERS: In a stunning development, it appears we may be trapped. I'll keep you updated as the story breaks. How was that? My hair look OK?

QUINCY THE CAMERAMAN: Gold, baby, gold.

JACKIE: So where are we?

REPETE: The Way Station. Half way to hopes and dreams.

JACKIE: So what time does the train come?

PETE: There is no train. Never has been.

LITTLE STEVIE: Are we stuck here? Forever? Huh? Are we? Huh?

JACKIE: No.

REPETE: Yes.

JACKIE: No. What are you two doing here?

REPETE: We work for Big Baby G.

JACKIE: Who?

PETE: You never heard of Big Baby G? He's a giant man. A giant.

CLAPPER: (Runs on.) Cue the giant! (Exits. A loud boom boom sound comes from Off-stage.)

REPETE: Oh man, that's him. You guys gotta hide. Big G doesn't like strangers down here. He's a bad, bad guy. Hide. (He helps them hide. The stagehands come out with a camouflage sheet and hold it between them about waist high. They ALL crouch behind it while PETE moves to intercept the giant. A huge voice. Loud stomping footsteps. Then BIG BABY G steps out. He's dressed like a rapper. Backwards hat, gold chains, baggy jeans.)

BIG BABY G: Yo. 'Sup dawg? Big Baby G is in da house.

PETE: Hey BBG. How you doin'?

BIG BABY G: Big Baby G is chillin' and thrillin' and killin and dillin' and … millin' and … um ah dang, man.

JACKIE: That's your giant?

REPETE: He's a huge man.

JACKIE: (Standing) He's like four feet tall!

REPETE: (Yanking her down into hiding) He's huge. He's gonna be the biggest rap artist in the world, man. Gigantor.

JACKIE: Oh please.

BIG BABY G: What was that?

PETE: Ah, nothing BG. How 'bout some dinner? Are you hungry? I could fix you a sandwich.

BIG BABY G: Big G heard somethin'. Fee fi fo fum, Big G smells the blood of an Englishman.

JACKIE: OK, that's just wrong. First of all we're not English, or men, and that doesn't even rhyme. Fum — man.

BIG BABY G: Big Baby knows he heard something that time. 'Bout a

49

rhyme bein' a crime. Gonna drop the time — (*He heads over to the hiding place but PETE is there to intercept and steer him back.*)

PETE: It's nothin'. Probably just the bats. Hey, how about some music?

BIG BABY G: Oh yeah, dawg. Why don't you go get my muse?

PETE: Sure thing BG. Muse, come on, you're needed.

CLAPPER: (*Runs On-stage.*) Cue the muse. (*Exits.*)

REPETE: Shhhh. (*And so the MUSE enters with a golden guitar. She doesn't look happy to be here.*)

PETE: Baby G wants to hear a song.

MUSE: Why?

BIG BABY G: 'Cause G got music in his soul, baby.

MUSE: No, you don't.

BIG BABY G: Yes, Big G do, it's true, just like you I sing the blues like my muse.

MUSE: You'll just take a sample of my song and talk over it.

PETE: Why don't you sing a lullaby?

MUSE: Why?

PETE: 'Cause maybe he needs to sleep. (*Wink-wink.*)

MUSE: No.

PETE: I really think you should. Others might be listening.

MUSE: No, I —

PETE: *Sing!* (*The MUSE starts to sing a lullaby. It's nice and soothing and pretty soon BIG BABY G is snoring lightly, fast asleep. ALL come out of hiding.*)

PETE: OK, he's asleep.

MUSE: Who are you?

JACKIE: Jackie. Who are you?

MUSE: I'm the muse that plays the golden records.

COW FRONT: Did she say moos?

COW BACK: Muse.

COW FRONT: Aw geez.

JACKIE: You're a songwriter?

MUSE: Yes.

JACKIE: Just like me. You're really good.

MUSE: Thanks.

JACKIE: What are you doing here?

MUSE: I'm stuck.

REPETE: Just like the rest of us.

JACKIE: But with your talent you could be huge.

MUSE: Maybe.

JACKIE: No maybe. I'm serious.

PETE: It doesn't matter.

REPETE: He's right. There's no way out of here.

JACKIE: There's gotta be a way out.

MUSE: No.

LITTLE STEVIE: Yeah, the escalator's gone.

PETE: And there's no train. This is it. We're stuck. (Sad music. JACKIE looks around. Moment of defeat. The DOOMCRYER comes out with his "End is Near" sandwich board. ALL hang their heads a moment. Then the DREAMWEAVER slips On-stage.)

DREAMWEAVER: So that's it, man. End of story. Like a lot of real life, sometimes you just hit a dead end. (Pause, then a sly wink.) 'Course, I told you, Jackie ain't no dummy. (Exits.)

JACKIE: (Lighting up) The tracks. The train tracks.

REPETE: Told you there is no train.

JACKIE: We don't need a train. Maybe that's the problem. You've all been sitting here, waiting for a free ride. Maybe there isn't one. Come on.

MUSE: But we don't know what's down there.

PETE: What if it's a dead end?

JACKIE: What if?

REPETE: What if we go down the wrong path? We could get lost. It's risky.

JACKIE: Yeah. But it's the only way to get where we're going. Who's with me?

LITTLE STEVIE: I am.

MAY WEATHERS: OK.

QUINCY THE CAMERAMAN: Gold, baby.

COW FRONT: Aw geez.

COW BACK: Yippee.

JACKIE: Are you coming with us? (Long moment as PETE, REPETE and the MUSE chew on this. Finally —)

PETE: OK.

REPETE: Alright.

MUSE: Yeah. But not without my guitar. (Goes to get the guitar, but BIG BABY G is sleeping on it. She gently pulls on it. He stirs. She pulls harder. He snorts. She yanks it free and thunk, his head hits the floor. He wakes up.)

BIG BABY G: Yo, 'sup dawg?

JACKIE: Run! (ALL go crazy. Everyone explodes into action, running around like headless chickens. BIG G is going for the guitar. It turns into a gigantic game of keep-away. Music is wild and fast as the chase goes on. More kids flood On-stage. It's wild and wacky. Primary kids are running all over stage. The REFEREE comes on shouting above the chaos.)

REFEREE: Flag on the play. Too many characters on stage. Illegal motions — whaaaa! (Gets swept aside in the chaos. Finally, JACKIE gets the guitar.)

JACKIE: I got it, let's go. (She leads them Off-stage.)

BIG BABY G: Wait. You can't go! You don't know where that leads!

Come back. (*But the lights begin to fade. DREAMWEAVER is there, talking to us again.*)

DREAMWEAVER: **So Jackie led the others into the darkness. They didn't know where they were going. Hey, man, who does? But they eventually found their way.** (*JACKIE and the others come out.*)

REPETE: **We made it.**

PETE: **I'd forgotten what sunlight was like.**

COW FRONT: **Mmmmm. Smell that fresh air.** (*His rear end smiles at him.*) **What?**

MAY WEATHERS: **This is May Weathers with a stunning development in a late breaking story.**

CLAPPER: (*Runs out.*) **And cue the criminal.** (*Exits.*)

FAST TOMMY: (*Comes out, suddenly seeing the crowd*) **Uh-oh.**

MAY WEATHERS: **This reporter is after a criminal.**

FAST TOMMY: **Yahhhh!** (*He turns and runs off.*)

JACKIE: **Let him go.**

LITTLE STEVIE: **But he cheated you. He said the chips would make your hopes and dreams come true.**

JACKIE: **I know.**

MUSE: **Here.** (*She tries to hand over the golden guitar.*)

JACKIE: **No. Thanks.**

MUSE: **Take it. It's got the power. It'll make you a great song writer.**

JACKIE: **That's just the point. I'd rather do it on my own.**

LITTLE STEVIE: **Jackie, I'm still hungry.**

JACKIE: **I know.**

LITTLE STEVIE: **And we still don't have any money.**

JACKIE: **I know.**

LITTLE STEVIE: **What are we gonna do? Huh? What?**

JACKIE: **I don't know.**

DREAMWEAVER: **And that's the story, yo. Ain't no simple answers here, man. Life in the big city don't always end with happily ever after. But you know what? Jackie ain't no dummy. So this one ends with happily mostly after. And outside of fairy tales, that's the way the story goes.**

So that's just one example of how you can take a story and twist it around and adapt it. If that is still just clear as mud, let's walk through another writing adventure.

Adapting the Story Part II

Step One – Tell the Story

Write down whatever you can remember.

The Emperor's New Clothes

Once upon a time there was this vain king who loved to try on lots and lots of royal robes. Some unscrupulous thieves decided to take advantage of the king's vanity. They said they could make a fabric that no one can see — if you couldn't see the material you're either stupid or incompetent. They sold this load of hooey to the king and his courtiers. Well, the king and his posse, who didn't want to look like idiots, pretended they could see the fabric. The evil dudes ran off with the king's real robes and most of his money. The king ended up in a parade, naked, where a little boy announced rather loudly, "The king isn't wearing anything." Moral: Through the mouths of babes can come truth, and I would also guess, vanity will get you every time. And possibly butt-naked in public usually ends in trouble.

OK, that's a pretty good summary, from memory, of the classic tale. But our goal is to make this play our own.

Step Two — Change the Components

Have the kids make suggestions as to what can change and write them on the board.

Step Three — Choosing Your Story

Here's what we decided for Finn's third grade class:

Hero — The Queen

Hero's Goal — A new heater for her undersea village. Her people were cold and in need of warmth.

Villain — Ninjas from an ice village

Setting — Under the sea

Time — Any

Obstacles — Following *The Emperor's New Clothes*, the Ninjas, who come from the land of ice, needed the heaters. While they were stealing them, they pretended to make the greatest heater in all the land, claiming the only ones who couldn't feel it are incompetent.

Outcome — One lone guppy admits that there's no heat and all learn from the innocence of a child.

Step Four — Writing Your Play

"Imagination is more important than knowledge."

— Albert Einstein

Creating Characters

You will need to create one character for each child and make sure each character has a name. Spear-carrier on the right won't do. But Bob, the spear-carrier on the right will make little happy, smiling faces.

Writing the First Page

The best place to start is with "Once upon a time," this way the audience knows it's a fairy tale. Other great openings are, "A long time ago," or "It was a dark and stormy night."

Once Upon a Time in Cindyland ...

I began with a Narrator.

Narrator 1: Once upon a time.

I wrote my first sentence. Yay for me. Time for a break. But I soldiered on.

OK, I knew I had to follow the structure of the original *Emperor*, so I had to meet the hero. Since I'd decided to make our hero a queen:

Narrator 1: Once upon a time there was a queen.

I wanted to learn something about her.

Narrator 1: Once upon a time there was a queen who loved being warm.

But why did she love being warm?

Narrator 1: Once upon a time there was a queen who loved being warm, for her land under the sea was cold.

Queen: Brrrr!

Oh boy, that's two lines. And on I went, inserting element "A" into plot point "B." Whenever I got stuck, I went back to the story to guide me, then I would ask "what if," and then "how." That primed my writing pump, opened up possibilities where none existed.

So back to my trusty Queen, I know she loved being warm 'cause her land was cold. What if she was a really rotten queen? Then she'd probably hoard the heaters. How? She'd store them in her dungeon. What if her people found out about the dungeon? How? Back and forth I went each time filling in the murky unknown. At the end I went back and rewrote the beginning, because by the time I got to the end, I knew where I should've started. It's always that way, isn't it?

For an example of an adaptation of the "Emperor's New Clothes," you can order Lauren Mayer's "Cool Suit" from Contemporary Drama Service.

Writing Your Own Show

Now is a good time to get out that vat of something caffeinated, and carve out a block of time for yourself. You'll find that once you start writing, you won't want to stop. Or you'll have a freshly painted garage. Up to you, really. Try to write if you can. I believe in you.

Writer Tips

"It took me fifteen years to discover that I had no talent for writing, but I couldn't give it up because by that time, I was too famous."

— Robert Benchley

"Writing is easy. All you do is stare at a blank sheet of paper until drops of blood form on your forehead."

— Gene Fowler

Believe

"One does not discover new lands without consenting to lost sight of the shore for a very long time."

— Andre Gide

Did you know that Peter Barsocchini was in his fifties when he wrote *High School Musical?* Did you know that Hemingway suffered ninety-seven rejections before he sold his first book? You can do this. First, write the story you want to adapt, just as you remember or think of it. Second, break down the components. Third, rebuild your story structure. Fourth, write it. Just remember to have fun along the way.

Cindy's TLC Tip #756

Immerse yourself in the world of your play. Have fun letting it "consume" you. What do I mean by that? If you're telling a tale of a princess or prince, oh for heaven's sake, go buy yourself a tiara or sword at a dollar store. Wear it as you write, or clean your garage, or dance around the living room. Eat your lunch on your fine china. Listen to classical music.

Once Upon a Time in Cindyland ...

When Flip and I were working on Disney's *Frankenstein* we became Bulgarian freaks. Well, not literally. But we had fun drinking our water out of beer steins. We ate meaty Kielbasa sandwiches on pumpernickel bread. We said "yah" und "nein" a lot to each other. We listened to German music. Sadly, the movie never got made. It was a little too dark for Disney. But I still have that beer stein — it's become a flowerpot with really great memories.

Chapter Five

Casting

"I don't want this part!"

It's time to cast or place your actors in their roles. This can be an arduous process.

You will need:

- Sides. *Sides* are scenes from your play featuring one, two, or sometimes more roles. They're your "cuttings" of the show, usually only the "larger" roles are put into sides. It's the script the little people will read from when they audition. It's not really necessary to do sides for all the characters.

Example of a side:

> JOE: I want this part.
> JIM: I want this part.
> JOE: But I deserve this part.
> JIM: I deserve it too.
> JOE: Why do you deserve it and I don't?
> JIM: 'Cause I wrote the show.

See? That has two characters, just a few sentences of dialogue, preferably a pivotal moment in the character's life so you can see if your actor has a range.

- Paper and pencils
- **The patience of Job** *

Cindy's System of Casting

After casting close to a hundred shows, most with actors younger than eighteen, I have found a system that works for me. It is not a perfect system. In fact, it's incredibly flawed, but it's the best of many systems we've tried. And seems to be the most fair.

Auditions Happen in Front of Everyone

When you are casting, insist that all actors who wish to have a role be present to watch. Do this for several reasons: it's a great learning tool for actors, they get to see how one person approached the role and decide if they want to be like it or do something very different, actors get to see the rest of the talent pool, sometimes this enables them to get past their own egos and realize there might be someone better for a role. If actors won't read in front of their peers, it's a fairly safe bet they're going to be the shy ones in front of an audience.

Before the first audition, hand out the paper and pencil to each actor. Tell them that you are giving them a chance to cast the show as well, offer a prize to the actor who casts closest to your choice. Do this because now, **"We're all in this together."** * * Everyone has a chance to walk a mile in your black boots; and when it comes time to announce the cast, some actors will actually be sympathetic to your plight of having to choose one person over another. [Note: I said *some* actors.] Also, by having everyone make a cast list, the kids now have something to do and you don't have to worry about their boredom factor kicking in.

Read Everyone

Odds are there are only four to six kids who speak above a whisper and are willing to read, the rest are adorable deer in the headlights, but this is theatre, a magical place that we want to make as fair as possible. So everyone reads. Let me repeat that, *everyone* gets a chance to read at least once.

After listening to all auditions, it's likely there are only one to three kids right for a role. You'll want to hear those kids read at least one more time for that part, but try different combinations of actors to find the right fit. If you're doing *Cinderella,* you wouldn't want to cast a forty-five-year-old Cindy and a twenty-two-year-old Prince, would you? (Or maybe you would — go Cinderella!)

Take notes of whom you liked and whom you didn't. Mark next to their names with a number system, simple exclamation points, copious thoughts, a yes or a no, whatever. The choice is yours. But do keep notes, because you'll need them when you sit down to cast, trust me.

Let Your Actors Choose If They'd Like to Read for Another Part

OK, you've got a general idea of how you'd like to cast. If time, I repeat *if time,* you can open it up to the actors. Is there any part they'd like to read for?

Every actor feels they can play every part. **Who said, "Actors are like children"?** * * * So give them a chance to prove that to you.

But word of warning here: give them a time limit — your time is valuable! Say, "OK, I have fifteen minutes, is there anyone here who would like to read for a role they *didn't* read for?" See how I said "*didn't* read for?" Yes, there are some children you really love, they're great kids, but they just can't play the role they want. As much as you'd like to give the kids a gazillion chances, you have to look out for the good of the show. Casting one child who is clearly not suited for a role because you care for him or her will not only hurt the child's confidence, but hurt the rest of your company. So as cruel as this sounds, cut everyone's losses and move on.

Once Upon a Time in Cindyland ...

We were doing our musical, *Quixote* (which is now available through Dramatic Publishing), an updated version of Cervantes' masterpiece *Don Quixote* that takes place in current day New Mexico. Alonzo, our hero, is a sixteen-year-old male. I kid you not, I had thirteen-year-old girls asking if they could read for that part. I had kids who have never sung before asking if they could read.

Call Backs

If you absolutely can't decide who to cast, then call back the actors you are uncertain about. Read them again — in the combinations you believe you want to cast. Read them once, twice tops, and then be done.

Once Upon a Time in Cindyland ...

I have agonized over casts. I have lost sleep over casting. And I have to say the worst casts I've had are because I didn't trust my guts. When we were doing our show, *Wild Dust: The Musical*, off Broadway, I had auditioned several women for the role of Sally. We had narrowed it down to a few actresses. One of them had credits up the wazoo and everyone told me she would be great for the part. Oh, and let me preface, I made this choice casting the Equity open audition style. *Equity* is the actor's union and their rule is that each actor comes in and is given three minutes to sing and read for you. That's it, three minutes. If you wish to see them again, you have to pay for a callback. So in three minutes I needed to decide if these actresses were right; I saw hundreds that day — yes, *day*. Anyway, something in me said I wanted to go with a friend of mine, Ann, back in L.A. Ann had originated the role when we did it as a straight play and was and still is one of the most talented actresses I have ever worked with. But she didn't have the credits. I went with the "logical" choice, the woman who'd done lots. What a nightmare she turned out to be. And she wasn't the only one. It was the most amazing thing I had ever experienced. Supposedly professional actors — actors who were being paid — could never remember their lines or blocking or lyrics. The stage manager actually had the gall to tell me, "Well, you can't expect these actresses to sing and dance at the same time." It was a nightmare, and one I'm sure won't happen to you, dear mommy, daddy, or teacher. After all, you're casting elementary school children, and I'm sure they'll be much better than that company.

Cast the Show

Word to the wise, do this the evening of the day you do auditions. *Don't procrastinate*. Sit down with all your notes and thoughts and make a list of your three top favorites for each role.

You will notice something here. A few of your actors are great for numerous roles, but there are one or two roles that have only one actor who can play it. Does that make sense? In other words, for one or two parts you'll know *exactly* who to cast, there will be five to ten roles that you have multiple choices for, and the rest of your parts you'll be scratching your head, wondering how you're going to cast.

I wish I had some sage words of wisdom to offer you here, but I don't. Do the best you can.

What I often do is ask my son, especially if he knows the kids. He's privy to that secret "kid" world. He knows who's mean on the blacktop, who gets their homework in on time, and the kids he can trust with a secret. I listen to his advice, and then trust my own intuition as much as possible. If you are a teacher, you may already know these things. If not, ask other teachers who may know these types of insights.

What I can tell you is that more times than not I've been pleasantly surprised. So keep your head up. And remember, even the professionals make mistakes, so it's no big deal if you cast wrong. During the recording of *The Lion King II*, a certain actress, who will remain unnamed, was cast as Kovu's mom. But she kept coming to the recording sessions a bit inebriated. Instead of saying "Kovu" she said, "Curevo." She didn't stay with the movie. Although you won't be faced with this particular problem, just keep your patience when you're trying to cast because you can always tweak things to better suit a character or actor.

Post Your Cast

Type up your cast sheet and go to bed. Sleep on it. Not literally, but you know what I mean. If in the morning it still feels right to you, then you can do this one of two ways: email it out to everyone, or you can tape it up to the MPR or classroom door. *Do not announce it.* This opens you up to a ton of headaches you do not want: crying kids, arguing kids, angry kids. And *do not announce* also means do not wait around to see little Susie or Johnnie's reaction. Hightail it out of there. Sing with me as you sneak off into the sunset ... **"It's all right now ... Ya can't please everyone, so ya just got to please yourself."** * * * *

Cindy's TLC Tip #297

You have done an amazing job. You sat patiently and listened hour after hour with a smile on your face and a song in your heart. It's time for you to get a little down time — off to a movie, you. Preferably, go see a guilty pleasure, but any film that looks fun will *do*. Have fun.

The Table Read

A table read is when your entire cast gets together, usually sitting around a table, and reads the script. This is exciting and nerve-wracking. Exciting because you get to actually hear the show with the actors you've chosen for the first time. Nerve-wracking because you get to hear the show with the actors you've chosen for the first time.

"I am Dying, Egypt, Dying" * * * * *

Word of dire warning here — there will be little ones with very broken hearts who will be unable to read because they didn't get the part they wanted. They will cry. They will sulk. They will give you that, "I don't care" look. You will need to address their feelings. You do this for so many reasons: first and foremost you care, you're a parent or teacher, you know what it's like to wipe away the tears of some little one you care about; you are building an ensemble so you need all the kids to be on this journey with you; and one lone voice of dissension can hurt a show tremendously.

Two stories here. The first to show you how bad things can get so *heed* my warning. The second will give you hope.

Once Upon a Time in Cindyland ...

I was working with my teen company doing our show *Usher* in L.A. I had a young woman who didn't like her role. But she wasn't there for "the talk" (see How to Mend the Broken Hearts on page 62) so these feelings never got addressed. As rehearsals progressed, she didn't care for the way I directed her — I actually asked her to look inside and use real emotions. She didn't like the way I disciplined. I insisted the kids clean up after themselves and that they be kind to others. Terrible, horrible requests as you can see. Well, she got to yapping to the other actors. Cussing at me behind my back. Directors do have their loyal followers which is how I knew about little Miss Potty-Mouth. Long story made longer, after several talks with her and her mother, I finally had to ask her to leave the show. The good of the one does not outweigh the good of the many.

Once Upon a Time in Cindyland ... continued

Then again, there are actors who light up the world. We were in New York to record *Lion King II* and James Earl Jones was coming in to record Mufasa. We were all excited with sweaty palms and everything. We suddenly realized that since Mufasa had died in the first film, he was only coming in to record the dream sequence. He had only one line. One line! You can't bring in James Earl Jones for one line. So the producer and the director asked us to write something. Flip had a plan. It was brilliant. We could write a monologue for him. I can still remember it now, "Flip and Cindy can't come to the phone right now, but if you'd like to leave a message" ... Turns out all our worry was for naught. Mr. Jones — who Flip still wants to be when he grows up — was the consummate professional. He actually told us he was open to line readings. *Line readings* are exactly how they sound, it's when you tell an actor, "Read it like this." But the thing is, you never tell an actor, "Read it like this." And you certainly don't tell Mr. Jones that. Not only that, he actually asked for our autograph for his granddaughter. Our autograph? Us? (Sigh.) Mr. Jones is the best.

How to Mend the Broken Hearts

OK, so now that I've gone down memory lane. Let's get back to how you're going to handle the broken hearts.

Step One — Listen to all of their complaints. Don't edit them or tell them, "Gee, it will be OK." Just let them say what they have to say. If there are tears, a hug here or there is in order.

Step Two — Acknowledge what you've heard. Respond to their feelings without fixing them. "I'm sorry you're sad," "I'm sorry you're disappointed," "I'm sorry this isn't what you want." You get the idea. And it may take a while. Patience, young master, patience.

Step Three — Let them hear your point of view. Explain that you are looking out for the entire show. You see things they cannot. And you believe you have cast the very best cast possible, 'cause you have! Then tell them the Jan Cohen story. It goes like this:

"When I went to high school we were doing our spring comedy. Jan got cast as the part of the secretary. She had three lines. Little, tiny lines, 'Yes, sir,' 'Yes, sir,' and 'Yes, sir.' Jan was brokenhearted because she'd gotten such a small part. But she threw herself into it. She created this fantastic character who was always dropping things and she was all hunchy — a real nervous hilarity with the Coke-bottle glasses to prove it. She was fantastic and she stole the show. The audience stood up and cheered for her when we came out for bows."

Now you don't know Jan Cohen, but maybe you do. If you do, tell her Cindy says "Hi." You can use the story to impart wisdom into your young thespians. Remind them there are no small parts, only small actors. Tell them they can take their part and really make it something, or just be sad and disappointed. Reassure them you believe they're going to be awesome in that part and if they just give it some time, they're going to find that they love it.

They will still be disappointed for the next rehearsal or two. But I have rarely seen a kid who didn't come around. So be patient.

Cindy's View of the World #701

Did you know that all those foods you thought were bad for you — jelly donuts, German chocolate cake, butter — actually become health food in your body when under stress? Mmmmhmmmm. Somehow, the food magically recomposes itself and has the same value as broccoli, so eat up!

Cindy's TLC Tip #54%

You have helped so many little ones drink hearty of life, how about you? I want you to go to the liquid section of your local market. And just look at all the different libations available to you. There's sparkling fruit juice soda, vitamin waters, deep burgundy wines, on and on the choices go. Now, buy one you haven't tried. Treat yourself to something that you've always wanted to taste. For me, it's those weird fruity drinks that Target sells, like Mango Kiwi Casaba Melon. If you're a beer drinker, try something outrageous. Like Klompermeirshien's Oktoberfest Stout Hearty Pale Ale Lager. But for heaven's sake, don't dump it into a paper cup. Make it a celebration. Get out the good glasses, the ones you only let company use. And now let me offer up a toast, "To you! You make this world a more delicious place!"

Let's Read

It's time to read the play. But don't just sit around and do that. You will need to break it up to make it fun. So use all your senses to do this. If you were doing *The Five Chinese Brothers*, bring in fortune cookies for everyone and then have them write their own fortunes. If you were doing a Hispanic adaptation of *Cinderella*, bring in some Latin music. Get up and dance a bit of Salsa with the kids.

This is the time for you to actually dust off those old cassette tapes or records and force your child or class to listen, oops, I mean expose your child or class to the music of your youth. Choose anything from Kool and The Gang to Meat Loaf (not the blue plate special, but the singer). Party on, dude! It's time to celebrate. You're going to put on a show.

Trivia Time

* **Job was the guy in the Bible who God tested, but Job never lost his faith.**

** **If you've been on a desert island or you come from another planet, you probably don't know that this song is from the first *High School Musical*.**

*** **"Actors are like children" was said by Alfred Hitchcock.**

**** **This song was sung by Ricky Nelson who wrote it after appearing at Madison Square Garden and getting berated for doing his new stuff. Ironicly, he wrote this in response and it became a huge hit for him.**

***** **"I am dying, Egypt, dying" was from The Bard's play, *Anthony and Cleopatra*. Mark Anthony utters these words to the Egyptian queen as he lies dying in her arms.**

Chapter Six

Blocking the Show

"I go where?!"

Blocking a show is like doing a jigsaw puzzle: you have a whole bunch of little shapes that you're going to shove together to create a really awesome picture. But before you can actually start putting your puzzle together, you've got to get organized. First you pull apart all the pieces and then set them with the color side up so you can see what's what. Then, if you grew up with my grandma, you have to pull out all the edges so you can build your frame. After that, you put it together.

That's how we're going to look at blocking your show. So let's begin with opening the box and seeing what's inside.

The Stage Layout

Did you know there are several different types of stages? Proscenium, horseshoe, and theatre-in-the-round? You can use any one of them as long as you understand what each stage layout can offer and what your challenges will be. Not only are there a plethora of theatre shapes to choose from, there's a huge vocabulary that we directors use — an ancient language passed on by the elders, you must pass an initiation test, which is difficult even for the purest of heart ... not really — up, down, center, and left — you'll learn it all.

Sit back, read, and know that when you are done with this chapter, you'll be so hip Mr. or Ms. Verbiage, that you'll be able to impress your friends at parties, faculty meetings, and PTSA meetings. "Hey, how's work?" "Well, Cin, I'm blocking completely up center on a horseshoe." OK, that sounded more impressive in my head. But you get the idea.

The Different Types of Stages
The Proscenium.

A proscenium has a raised stage at one end of the building, the audience sits on the other, and there's a proscenium arch, which separates the actors from their audience. Think of a traditional theatre. There are loads-o-benefits to this kind of layout: it's versatile, it's easy to block because all your actors are in one place, and it's traditional, so your audience feels pretty safe with the arrangement. But if you're looking to do something off the beaten path, then this might not be right for you. Also, the kids really have to project so that their sweet, little voices can be heard across the distance, unless you're blessed with microphones.

The Horseshoe

The horseshoe, or thrust, is pretty much like it sounds. Your audience surrounds the stage on three sides. Usually, the stage is on the floor and the audience is elevated so they can comfortably see the action. This type of theatre set-up is great if you're looking for intimacy; you want your audience to feel more "connected" to the play. The challenge with this type of layout is in blocking. You've got to make sure your actors aren't showing their backs, most of the little faces have to be seen — most of the time.

Theatre-in-the-Round

Theatre-in-the-round is where the audience surrounds the stage on four sides. Again, the audience is usually elevated a bit to make sure they can catch the action. This type of theatre is way cool if you want to do something "environmental," actors move in, out, and through the audience. The difficulty of this type of theatre is, again, staging. You have to make sure that actor's faces are seen and you've got interesting traffic patterns.

Traffic patterns are the entrances and exits of your actors. You don't want them all coming in from the same side of the stage, you want them coming in from the left and right and up and down. That makes it more fun for the audience and keeps the play moving.

Blackbox

This is just like it sounds, a big black box to be shaped as you, the director, sees fit. There are no planted seats or sets; everything is mobile, which makes it fun to do really avant-garde theatre.

To Sum it Up

So why is it necessary to know all the different stages when you're stuck with an MPR or a classroom? Maybe you're doing a little guy's adaptation of *A Midsummer Night's Dream* and you envision your little fairies flitting through the audience. Or maybe you're creating a production of *Cinderella*, and your audience is mostly children under five, you might want to keep your audience "safe" from dirt-stained hands.

Your staging is only as limited as your imagination, any space can be magically transformed.

Once Upon a Time in Cindyland ...

When we were putting on our L.A. production of *Wild Dust,* we didn't have a theatre. So we had to create one from a catering hall. Yep, a catering hall that had been a movie theatre some years back. We were able to build a proscenium stage, but we had sound problems because of the vastness of the space. So we turned it into a horseshoe (you now know what that means, don't you?). With the audience on three sides, I had my work cut out for me, and they were better able to hear.

Another time, we worked at a wonderful little theatre called The Hub in North Hollywood — sadly, it no longer exists. But anyway, it was a forty-seat space with a proscenium stage the size of a shoebox, (I'm exaggerating, it was actually twelve feet by twelve feet) and we were working with thirty teens — do the math. There just wasn't room for every kid on that stage. We turned it into theatre-in-the-round. I used every part of that space I could think of — including the bathroom for entrances and exits. Actually, I think the audience ended up liking the "intimacy." They said they felt like they became part of the story instead of just distant observers. This also helped with sound problems, because there was a karaoke sushi bar that would kick on its music every night at 8:00 pm — loudly — but that's another story.

So you can transform any space, including a garage, into a theatre. Never let where you're working stop you from creating your dream piece of theatre.

The Different Types of Words

"Just know your lines and don't bump into any furniture."

— Nigel Rees

Stage left. Upstage right. Center. These are terms you and your little actor people will become familiar with, prior to actually getting the show up on its feet. Why not just say, "Move over there?" Well, first of all, where is *there?* We all need a common language. And second, what fun is that? You want to sound hip and cool and know the lingo, right?

OK, we're going to learn our vocabulary with a proscenium in mind. Actors are standing in front of you, expecting you to move them around. Where do they go?

Upstage: If they were walking away from you, towards the back wall, they'd be heading "up the stage" or up and away from you. In the golden-olden days of theatre, stages were literally *raked,* meaning the back of the stage was higher than the front of the stage. Like a very subtle ramp. Hence the term, "Upstage," meant to move up.

Downstage: If they were to walk toward the audience, they'd be walking downstage, because they are walking down the ramp.

Center stage: * That's exactly like it sounds, the very center of the stage.

Easy so far, right?

Now about left and right. Since the actors are doing the moving around, and not you, they need to understand things from their vantage point. In other words, our job is to make it as simple for them as possible; you must think in terms of the "actor's right," or the "actor's left." Everything becomes opposite for you. For an actor to move "Down right," they would move towards the audience, but to *your* left. If you want them to move "Up left," they'll move towards the back wall but to *your* right.

But wait, there's more.

We directors never say, "move over there." No, why would we? It's simple and familiar. We have our own lingo for that as well. We say "cross," which means "move" but somehow sounds niftier.

All right, let's recap. Down is towards you and up is to the back wall. Left is actor's left and right is actors' right. When you want your actors to go anywhere, you say, "cross."

Now, you're going to need to keep track of all of this in your script, because trust me, actors do not remember. Even when they write it down and you repeat it many times, they seem to forget. So you are going to need a code of some kind, something simple and quick to keep track of where everyone is crossing. I usually use the "X" system. Example: if I want an actor to cross down left, I would write, "XDL;" the X is for the cross, the "D" is for down, and the "L" is for left. When things really get cookin' I'll do something like, XLofCIND. This means I want the actor to cross the stage and stand on the left of Cinderella.

Actually, the kids really love this part of learning theatre, because to them it's like a game.

The Blocking Game

I love this game for so many reasons: it's a fun way to teach spatial relationships (can you believe it, theatre even improves their math skills. Amazing.), it teaches the kids cooperation and leadership, and it's just darn fun.

You will need:

• A dry erase board and pens, or a chalkboard and chalk

• A sharpened pencil for each child

First, explain to the kids about up, down, and center. Then explain to them about actor's left and right. They're pretty smart little beings, they get it quickly.

Second, ask for volunteers. The child then goes up onto the stage. Tell them where you want them to go, "Down left," "Up right." Do this until each child has had their turn to go somewhere on stage. Once your entire company is up there, have them cross from place to place. Word of warning here, if your company is bigger than, say, twenty-five, do this in groups of under fifteen. It can get confusing.

Have the children sit back down.

It's their turn to "play director." Again, ask for volunteers. One child will be the "director" and one will be the "actor." The "director" tells the "actor" where on stage to go. Give each child a turn or two, depending on how much time you have.

Have the children sit back down.

It's time for them to learn how to write the code in their scripts. Explain to them the "X" system. Write a few examples on the board. Ask for a volunteer. Give that child a stage direction and then ask them to write it on the board. Do that for a few times and then let the children play director again. One child gives the direction; one child writes it down.

This game rocks. It lets them write on the board and learn stage directions, How cool is that?

Finally, give each child their "honorary" pencil, for they have "officially" entered the world of "actor." Tell them they mustn't lose their pencil, for it's a very powerful tool and will help them along their journey to "performer." An ordinary pencil, which they will need at every rehearsal, is now powerful in its own right. **"The pen is mightier than the sword"**** has become an important and symbolic tool for them. Ah, the amazing things theatre can do.

Cindy's TLC Tip #8

You've "come of age," too, you know. You need a symbolic gesture. Go out and buy yourself a binder, the kind with the plastic front and back that you can stick pictures in. This is your "official" director's book. Three-hole-punch your script and place it inside. Now, it's time to decorate your book. First, do a title page. And don't be stingy with the colors or the stickers or the fonts. Make it exactly as you like. You can even print your title page on expensive paper. Whatever you wish. Now slide your title page behind the front plastic cover. Second, fill the back cover with quotes and pictures that inspire you. Congratulations, Grasshopper, you are now a director.

Creating Pictures

A director's job is to paint pictures for the audience. You do this by making sure you are telling the story in a way that the author intended, helping your actors to find the emotional truths for the characters they are playing, and placing your actors in attractive "tableaus" on the stage. That's a hoity-toity way of saying you matter, dude. You're the interpreter of the play and you have got to use every tool at your disposal to make sure the audience understands what the author was trying to convey.

Traffic Patterns

Just like cruising down the highway, You're rolling down the freeway of your show. All entrances and exits need to run smoothly. You don't want all your actors coming on from the same place, or They'll get bottlenecked. You don't want them to move around haphazardly, or there will be accidents. You need to guide the actors on and off the stage.

So the first thing to do when you're ready to block your show is the traffic patterns. Go through the entire play just doing the entrances and exits of your characters. When do they come on and when do they leave? Where do they come on and where do they leave? Then run through the show and take a look at it. Is there enough flow? Are you using enough of the entrances and exits available to you?

Finding Focus

If you're happy with your traffic, then it's time to *focus* the movement. Like a lens of a camera, you want your audience to see one thing and to see it clearly. That's what focus is all about.

Oftentimes there are many people on-stage, but only one speaking. It's your job to make sure the actor yakking away up there is being heard and noticed. So you block with that in mind. You might tell the rest of the actors, the ones not speaking on-stage, to use very small gestures, you can ask them to freeze, you can dim the lighting on them and slam a spot on your guy speaking, and you can place the rest of the actors around your speaking character in a way that makes the audience look at him or her. All of these will assist focus.

These two actually loved butting heads — in and out of the show. But that chemistry paid off. Aren't they cute? Aside from looking cute, the attention of the audience is drawn to this physical action.

Creating Levels

OK, so we know that we're going to focus our scene, but where does the scene take place? Well, of course, there's the right, left, up, and down part of your stage. But that can get pretty boring for the audience after awhile. It's up to you to create "levels." Now, if you're lucky, you'll have the budget for platforms, but sometimes you don't and you've got to create heights using nothing but your imagination. How do you do this?

Characters can stand shortest to tallest or tallest to shortest or they can stand in semi-circles, V-shaped patterns, on chairs, on tables, and they can kneel or sit on the stage. They can lay down, they can lean on things, and they can bend. The choices are endless. Just remember, you're the interpreter of the play. It's up to you to keep the intent of the author in mind.

Here's an example: You have an aggressive character. He's the leader of the pack and everyone follows him. But through the course of your play he changes. He realizes that he has been unfair and wants everyone to work together in harmony. So, at the beginning of the show, if you have platforms, you might have him do a lot of his scenes on the top platform, towering over everyone else. But by the end, he's working on the stage floor with everyone else, no longer above the crowd, but part of it. If you don't have levels, you might have a chair or two. His chair is the big wingback while all his flunkies sit in kindergarten classroom chairs. You see? We're painting pictures for the audience. We didn't come out with a neon sign that said, "This guy is a leader." We showed them through the pictures we created.

Trust Yourself

There is no right or wrong when directing. There is only your eye and what looks best to you. And most times it's trial and error. Rob Reiner, who directed one of my very favorite movies, *An American President*, said that he didn't know the movie he wanted to make until it was finished and in the can. You've got to experiment. See what works.

Map It Out

A lot of directors I know "think on their feet." I don't. That thought terrifies me, especially when working with a passel of little people who can turn savage at any moment and I'm all out of raw meat and tranquilizer darts. Come in prepared. Know where you want your actors to go and have a vague picture of how you wish them to stand. You can change it. You can rearrange it. You can throw it all away. But if you don't know where you're going when you walk in, within minutes you will get lost. And we like you. We need you. We want you around, with all the pretty hair on your head.

Cindy's View of the World #92F

Actually, this is my friend Domenic's view of the world, but I think it applies. And it has given me creative freedom more times than I can count. "Dare to Suck." Don't worry about being perfect. Take the risk. Live! Make mistakes. You're bound to find what you're looking for by walking down that rocky road. And who knows? You might find something even better.

It's a Wrap

Let's review the vocabulary words:

- Blocking: actors moving around the stage, hopefully in some pretty patterns
- Proscenium: stage on one side, audience on the other, an arch to separate the two
- Horseshoe or Thrust: audience surrounds the stage on three sides, like a horseshoe
- In the Round: audience surrounds the stage on all four sides
- Blackbox: a big, black box of a space where everything is movable
- Crossing: moving across the stage from one place to the other
- Left: your right
- Right: your left
- Center: the center of the stage
- Up: move towards the back wall or away from you
- Down: move towards the audience or towards you
- Traffic Patterns: the entrances and exits of your actors
- Focus: where to have the audience look on stage

Good job, you've learned your vocabulary. Now here's just a little test for you.

XDL is _____

XUR is _____

XC is_____

Trivia Time

* ***Center Stage*** **was a movie about the American Ballet Academy. It is a total guilty pleasure with the most implausible, but wonderful dance sequence at the end. If you like dance movies, rent it. It's great fun.**

* * **"The pen is mightier than the sword," was a phrase coined in 1839 by Edward Lytton, used in his play, *Richelieu, or the Other Conspiracy.***

Chapter Seven

Recruiting and Backstage Fun

"Hey Mom, my director wanted me to give you this paper."

Since no one should have this much fun alone, you will want to find a crew. The best place to look is to your cast because they all have naïve, but eager parents. At the back of this chapter you will find many forms. The Volunteer Questionnaire form on page 84 is one of many useful forms. Use this once the show has been cast. Send this form home with your little actors. Many parents will toss it away, hoping you won't find them, but there are a few out there who will offer their help. Take them up on it. Repeat after me, "Yes, thank you. That would be wonderful." You cannot get enough assistance!

The Crews

In a perfect world, there are crew heads and lots of volunteers for each crew. But what exactly do the crews do?

Excellent question, Grasshopper. Let's look, shall we?

The Stage Manager

The stage manager is the director's right hand. This lovely person is beside you every step of the way, starting when you block the show right on through to the strike. The stage manager writes the blocking down and follows the script to make sure the actors stay *on book* — saying the words as they're written in the script and not making up lines or quoting from a *Green Acres* episode. They *call* the show — tells everyone where they're suppose to be during the performances. And they run the *strike* — tearing the set down.

They lead the *running crew,* which is a team that works backstage during the show. They handle sets and set changes and wrangling of the kids, keeping the little ones quiet and making sure they're not off stampeding the playground.

Costume Designer

This person figures out what everyone will be wearing. But they don't run off willy nilly, first they read the script, then meet with the director so everyone is on the same page. You don't want a director who envisions everyone in full medieval garb and a costume designer who thinks they'd all look better in Roy Rogers' fringe. Once the basic concept for the costumes has been decided, the costume designer will beg, borrow, or make whatever is needed. Notice I didn't say steal.

Their team is *wardrobe*, they make sure actors' costumes are clean and ready when and where the actors need them. *Wardrobe* is anything the actors "wear."

Costume Hints

Once the costume has been obtained, hang it in the dressing room, if you're lucky enough to have one, with the child's name taped to it. Use masking tape. If you don't have a dressing room, put it in a paper bag with the child's name on it so it's easily transportable. *Do not send the child home with it!* If you must, keep them in your garage or car trunk or bedroom.

Last note about costumes: Keep the kids as involved as possible. One costume design that I have done many times and found hugely successful is jeans — every child has a pair or they can be easily borrowed — and simple white T-shirt. Add on a costume piece or two to symbolize the character: a crown and wand for a queen, a beard for an old wizard, or a tail for a dog. You've got yourself a very kid-friendly costume.

Costume Craft

You will need:

• The kids' white T-shirts

• Fabric paint in a rainbow hue

Paint the white T-shirts with fabric paint. Little actors can paint: what they believe their character would wear, or the words their character says, or what they think the show is about. Not only is this a great way to keep little hands and minds busy while you're working with other actors, but the kids have an awesome memento of the show.

Cindy's View of the World #30

K.I.S.S. Keep it simple, silly. It's so easy to go grandiose with your plans. Whenever I start a show, I envision it becoming a full scale Broadway production with orchestral score and Tony Awards*. But then the reality of time, money, and the fact that I'm working with little children sets in. And I realize the best thing I can do is K.I.S.S.

Prop Master

Similar to the costume designer, but this dude figures out what props are needed and gathers them. *Props* are the items held by the cast during the show: a pen, a knife, a book, or a tree branch. It can get kinda weird sometimes. Imagine a sword. Is that part of costumes or props? Well, if it's just worn as decoration, it's probably a costume. If it's taken out, it's a prop. There is some overlap between departments. Most times the costume designer and the prop master can agree before it becomes a fist fight. If that occurs, I recommend best two out of three falls.

The *prop department* takes care of props during the show. They do this by creating a prop table, which is a large table, shelf, or space where all the props are stored and marked so actors can grab them when needed. The prop department also makes sure everything is returned to its proper spot during and after the show. Covering the table with butcher paper, or whatever construction paper sheets the school has to offer, can really help. This way you can draw a square around each prop and label it, that way it only takes a glance at the table to realize something is missing.

Set Designer

The set designer designs the set, with the director's approval. Together, the two of you will determine how many levels and entrances you'll need and what kind of furniture, if any, will be used.

The *set crew* helps the designer build the sets.

Set Craft

You will need:

• Colored pens

• Paper

Step One — Have each child draw pictures of what they think should be on the flats. Let them go hog wild. Don't limit them. They can draw sea serpents, space ships, and castles. Whatever they dream.

Step Two — Have the kids paint the flats in a neutral color: pale white, cream, or beige. Whatever used paint or half gallons you have laying around from the bathroom you painted five years ago. Whatever. Make sure the kids are wearing smocks or clothes that they can ruin and you have lots of drop cloths to protect the floor. Make sure only a few little ones work at a time.

Step Three — Transfer the kids' images, in jumbo size, to your flats. Don't worry if you're not an artist. Remember, this is a children's set, the audience isn't looking for perfection. They will love, love, love seeing their child's artwork up on the stage. But if drawing really intimidates you, you must know someone who knows someone who can sketch it out for you. If not, Flip likes to scan the pictures onto his computer, then print them out on transparencies. You can get these at any office supply store. Then he borrows the school's overhead

This is an example of completed flats. I pulled my hair out because kids like to paint everything, including themselves and each other.

projector to project the image onto the flats. Then it's just a matter of tracing. This really captures the kids' designs.

Just remember, draw everything in pencil first.

Step Four — Outline each of the images in black paint. If you use a black marker, like a Sharpie, you will permanently "stain" your flat, so don't. Flats are reusable. A Sharpie mark will magically pop through the paint time and again. Twenty coats of paint won't hide a Sharpie.

Step Five — Take the flats back to the kids and have them paint the images. Make sure they're wearing smocks *and* you have plenty of drop cloths *and* only have a few kids do it at a time.

Step Six — Voilà, stand back and admire your flats.

Makeup and Hair Designer

Just like it implies, this person decides the hair and makeup design for each actor. Often they show the actor how to put their makeup on, unless you're lucky enough to have a team of volunteers.

House Manager

The house manager runs the *house*, or the area where the audience will be. They make sure there are programs and tickets to disperse and money for change.

Ushers are on their team. They take tickets, give out programs, and seat the audience.

House Hints

Tickets will need to be printed up. This is so easy. Most Word programs should have a template for business cards. Just open that template, fill in the information for your show. Voilà, you can print up ten tickets per page.

Programs will also need to be printed, but remember Cindy's View of the World 3Q. K.I.S.S. In your program, include cast members and the characters they play — please, oh please, do this in alphabetical order or in order of appearance and not by size of role. You'll also have your crew credits — that's everyone who had anything to do with making this production work, including you. Special thank yous are always appreciated. Include the principal whether you felt their help or not, because it makes for happy relations down the pike. Finally, write a smitch about the story and your journey getting here and call it, "From the Director."

Some productions go nutty on their programs. They have cast pictures, notes from families, and ads. That's all well and good if you have the time to coordinate that, it can be a moneymaker for you. It's up to you.

Program Craft

You will need:

- Pens in a plethora of colors
- 8 ½" X 11" paper

Step One — Fold the paper in half so it's now 5 ½" x 8 ½".

Step Two — Have the kids draw their version of the program on the front half of the paper so it's like the cover of a book. Again, let them have loads-o-fun with this. What is their concept for the show? I've seen kids with smaller parts draw a huge picture of their character with token guest appearances by everyone else. Oh, make sure the kids sign their names on the front cover.

Step Three — Xerox *all of them* on pretty colored paper.

Step Four — Insert the information about who's who inside.

Step Five — Pass them out at performance. Listen to the "oooohs" and "aaaahs" and "isn't that cute?" Watch the parents "fight" over getting their own kid's drawing.

Lighting/Sound Designer

This is the person who determines the kind of lighting and sound the show will need. They figure out things like microphones, sound effects, types of lights needed, where the lights will be set, and when they'll be needed. Again, they must answer to the director.

Lighting and sound crew set the lights and levels for the sound. They then run all the sound and light cues once the show is in production.

If you wish to learn more about the different jobs and the specific things each one brings to the production table, there are many books out there. Just go to Amazon.com and type in "Theatre." Also, many junior colleges offer inexpensive classes in technical design and production.

Crew Forms

"We got to get organized, we got to get smart..." * *

Right now, things are pretty calm in "showland," but in a few weeks it's going to get crazy. And you want to stay on top of it. Each crew chief will be helped with the use of forms. Forms help everyone be on the same page and keep things organized. Your crew chiefs should have three copies: one for him or her, one for the stage manager, and one for you, oh brilliant and courageous director. You should create a special section in your "Director's Book," to put all of them.

You can create the forms yourself, or you can use the ones at the end of the chapter.

Once Upon a Time in Cindyland ...

We were doing *Wild Dust: The Musical* in Florida. I was doing a run-through of the show, but it was a *shotgun,* a speedy run-through. The actors were pacing across the stage while they said their lines. One of my actresses decided to close her eyes while she did this, I kid you not. She walked into the orchestra pit and twisted her ankle.

The Production Team's Forms

These forms are about all the legal mumbo jumbo. Thankfully, in my entire career of doing this, I have only needed to use all this information once.

The production team forms are at the end of the chapter. See page 85 for the Emergency Form, page 84 for the Child Photo Parental Release form, page 86 for the Emergency Protocol Guidelines, page 87 for the Suggested Performance Guidelines, and page 88 for the Community Emergency Telephone Numbers.

Reading the Forms

The production forms are self-explanatory.

Once Upon a Time in Cindyland ...

My very favorite costume designer in all the land is a woman named Mickey Bronson. Mickey is this beautiful, petite German woman who is younger than her years. She's creative and brilliant, but she's also human. We were doing our musical, *Nottingham* (available through Pioneer Drama) and there were forty kids in the cast. Each kid had one or two changes, plus we were doing another show at that time, *Bard High,* with more kids and more costume changes. Mickey thought she was going to lose her mind. She and I had a terrible, tearful fight because it was so unorganized. This form was born out of that war. Thankfully, Mickey and I worked it out. And she is still my costume designer of choice. And my friend.

The Costume Team's Form

With up to sixty children, and possibly more than one costume change, keeping track of who gets what can drive you mad.

Reading the Form

The Costume List (see page 89) form is pretty self-explanatory, but here are the explanations just in case.

Character Description is for your designer's notes. They won't have to keep it in their head nor keep asking you; they just have to refer to the form.

Actor's Name and Sizes makes life simpler for those many Goodwill excursions.

Borrowed From is just like it sounds. If you borrowed, who from?

Prop Teams' Form

There are two different kinds of props: the handheld and the set prop. The *handheld* is the one the actor actually holds and uses as part of the action of your play. The *set prop* is stage dressing: books in the bookcase, food in the kitchen, snow needed to fall for a later scene.

Reading the Form

See General Prop List on page 90.

Borrow is exactly as it sounds. If you borrowed it, from whom did you borrow it? Knowing this will make it so much easier to return the props when the show is over. Remember, you're going to be wanted back next year! And you don't want Johnny's 350 pound father knocking on your door, demanding to know why no one returned his $2,000 telescope he so kindly lent you.

Buy and Make indicate that you are going to have to buy the prop or make it. And then who is going to do this?

Set Teams' Form

This is less of a form and more an instruction guide. See How to Build a Simple Flat on page 83.

Your set will need *flats*. Flats are stage walls. They give your stage depth and interest and a place to hide the little children before they come on.

How many flats? That's completely up to you and your designer.

What? You don't have a designer. No worries. You have a friend, or a neighbor, or an unsuspecting husband or wife who would be willing to put it together for you. Remember, the one thing schools have in abundance is manpower. Odds are someone at your school is a general contractor, or handyman, or at least knows which side of the hammer is the bangy part.

Makeup and Hair Team's Form

This form tells the makeup team who is getting what kind of makeup and what is needed. Little Billy needs a long white beard. Charlie needs a duck's bill. I wish you and Charlie good luck with that.

Reading the Form

See Makeup/Hair List on page 91.

Character Description is a description of the character.

The *Actor* means what child is playing what role.

Makeup and Hair Description means what does the hair and makeup for the character look like. Princess Tiffany needs long eyelashes, big red lips, and glitter on her cheeks.

The *Needed* column indicates whether you have the long false eyelashes and glitter, or you need to go buy those items.

Who is Doing means who is responsible for that child's makeup. Is it the makeup team? The child's parent, aunt, or giddy grandma, or is the kid doing it themselves?

House Forms

Any time money changes hands, it's really important to keep records. So you want to track your ticket sales. I cannot stress this enough. There are two forms to help you do this.

The Ticket Checkout form, see page 92, is used in the weeks prior to performance when you hope your cast and crew are out there selling tickets. But you have to keep records of who has taken tickets, how many, and did they return them. You don't want to oversell. You don't want tickets floating out in the ethers.

The Ticket Sales form, see page 93, is for the performance nights. When people come to the door and buy their tickets, you'll need a form to keep track. Some parents will do *Will Call*, which is asking you to hold the tickets but pay at the door. It's your basic nightmare, but *es muy importante,* so try to accommodate.

Reading the Forms

In the Ticket Checkout form, the *Given To* and *Phone Number* means who did you give those tickets to and their phone number in case you need to contact them. An e-mail address will also work. *How Many* is how many tickets were given out. Most house managers will want to number the tickets in order to help track how many tickets have been given out and who has them, which is the *Ticket Numbers* column. Remember, tickets equal money. Numbers also help when showtime comes. If you know that numbers forty-five to fifty haven't shown up yet, you might want to hold the curtain. *Date Paid/Date Returned* references tickets that have come back. For instance, if you gave little Jimmy tickets seventy-five through eighty-five and he sold only five tickets, mark down the date he returned tickets eighty-one through eighty-five. If he brought in a check for the sold tickets, mark that date. *Total* refers to the amount of money you have in your hot little hands versus the amount of tickets out in the ethers.

The Ticket Sales form is pretty self-explanatory. *How Many* refers to how many tickets sold. *Date Paid* can let you know if they plan on paying at the door. *Total* is once again the cold hard cash or check in your hands.

Lighting and Sound Teams' Forms

I think lighting a show is one of my favorite things to do. It really can create a mood. Sound and music can fill in the nuances of your show. They are "loverly." If you don't know how to hang a light, or handle a board, there is usually some techno parent who is more than happy to lend a hand. If you find one, they are usually an enthusiastic human who will go hog wild. Oh, let them. If, however, you don't have anyone, no worries. Parents are incredibly forgiving people as long as you've given their little pumpkin a moment in the sun, where they're free to blind everyone with their flash.

Reading the Form

See Lighting and Sound Cues on page 94.

This form is pretty easy to understand. *Cue or Dialogue* means what is being said prior to the light change. *CHRCR* is the character who is saying the line. The *Light and Sound Cue* means, is it a light cue or a sound cue or maybe it's both? Notes might be "bring this up hard and fast" or "fade this light out."

A Happy Crew is a Happy ... Crew

Sadly, we don't live in a perfect world. We live in a place where everyone is busy with little time to help out, so you may be lucky to get one or two parents who do all the jobs. Because you need them, it's important to treat them very well.

Cindy's TLC Tip #2.2

It's pedicure time for you and your crew. What better place to discuss costume and set needs than at a salon? The nail polishes will give you ideas for the color palette of your show. If you and your crew are a bunch of males, how about making it "Miller Time"?

It's a Wrap

You probably now know more than you ever wanted to know about what goes into a production. You've learned how many possible jobs there are. Do you need all of these people to put on a production with all the bells and whistles of lights and sound and makeup? Heavens, no! You need a handful of willing parents and a barrel of heartfelt appreciation. That's it.

Remember to say please and thank you. Remember to say it a lot. And there's no harm in bringing in a treat every now and then. Chocolate chip cookies and juice can go a long way in tempering a cranky company.

Once Upon a Time in Cindyland ...

When we did *The Queen's New Heater* with my son's third grade class, we had a series of mishaps. At the start of one performance, the curtain didn't open wide enough, the mics went out, and one of our flats fell during the performance. Yep, tumbled onto a kid's head. Thankfully, little Natalie was a trouper and she wasn't hurt. The show went on. Actually, I stepped out and said, "If we were taping this, we'd rewind. So that's what we're gonna do. Start again." And we did. Now, I wouldn't ordinarily recommend you step out during a show. Gosh, **the show must always go on***. But this was an educational experience for the kids and I wanted them to see that we can make mistakes and still laugh and have fun. Which is what we did. And here's the neat part, the audience did, too. Mistakes, no lighting, no budget — the audience still had a good time.

Trivia Time

*The Tony Awards, whose hoity-toity real name is the Antoinette Perry Awards for Theatre Excellence acknowledges excellence in American Theatre with a ceremony in New York.

** "We gotta get organized..." is a lyric from one of my favorite musicals, *Cotton Patch Gospel* by Harry Chapin.

*** "The show must go on," is a song by English rock band Queen. It's the final track of their 1991 album, *Innuendo*. The song chronicles the effort of Freddie Murphy continuing to perform despite the impending end of his life.

How to Build a Simple Flat

Flats can be built quickly and easily using readily available materials. At one time, flats were made with cloth, muslin, or canvas stretched across wooden frames. This required the framework to be braced at the corners, making construction more complicated and time consuming. The simple technique described below will provide sturdy flats for the least investment in time and money.

Each flat will require four, 8-foot 1x2's. You may also use 1x3's or 1x4's if you wish to have a deeper frame — this makes it a bit easier to attach the flats together later. However, standard 1x2's — also known as furring strips — will save the most money. The actual dimensions of a 1x2 are ¾" by 1¾", just as a modern 2x4 is actually 1½" by 3½". This is important for measuring the length of the shorter pieces of the frame.

Each flat will also require a 4-foot by 8-foot sheet of luan plywood. These are available at any lumber or home improvement warehouse store. The small sheets (3'x7') are called doorskins. Be sure to get the 4'x8' size. In addition to the 1x2's and 4'x8' sheets of plywood, you will need sixteen 1½" wood or drywall screws for each flat, plus some wood glue and a staple gun.

To begin, cut two 1x2's to exactly 8-feet long, if they're not already pre-cut to exact dimensions. Next, cut the other two 1x2's into four pieces, each exactly 3 feet, 10½ inches long. Arrange the pieces of cut wood as shown. Be sure the narrow (¾ inch) sides are resting flat

on the workbench or floor. Apply glue at the joints and use two screws at each joint to attach the pieces together (drilling pilot holes smaller than the screws will make this easier). Once the frame is complete, it will still flex a bit. This problem will be solved with the next step.

Cover the frame with the sheet of luan. Starting on one corner (this is important), begin stapling the sheet to the long 8-foot side of the frame, making sure the edges of the frame are smooth and flush before stapling. When the long side is done, begin from that corner and line up the short side before stapling. The frame will now be square and even. Finish stapling around the edges. To locate the crossbars for stapling, mark the edges of the luan where the screw heads show on the sides of the frame, then use a straight edge to draw pencil lines across the sheet of luan. The flat is now complete and ready for painting. To attach flats together, simply screw through the sides of the frames where they join.

Painting the flats can be done inexpensively using surplus paint. Old, half-empty paint cans may be found in parents' garages. Hardware stores and warehouses often have paint that was mixed wrong for sale. Any light color will do as base coat, and luan will soak up a lot of paint on the first coat. The light colored base coat will provide a background for scene-specific painting done later.

3 feet, 10½ inches

8 feet

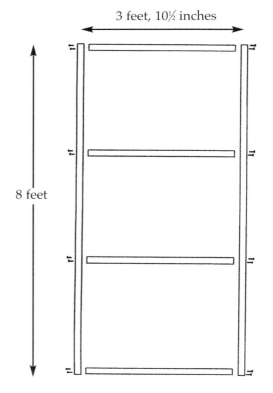

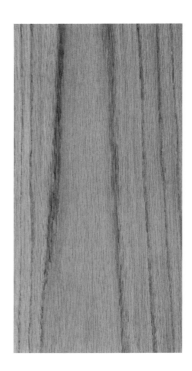

Volunteer Questionnaire

The school play production does not just happen. It is the result of thousands of man-hours in not only musical preparation, but in construction, painting, decorating, ushering, and many other activities. The help and assistance is most necessary. The production needs you!

We are asking each parent to commit to some area of service. If you are not physically able to help, your commitment of audience support would be invaluable. Please complete the portion below and place it in the indicated box, located in the Principal's office, to let us know how you may be able to help in this strategic outreach of our school.

Name:_____

Phone Numbers: (Home) _____ (Cell) _____

E-mail: _____

Circle Category of Interest:

Costumes	Childcare	Cleanup
Food	House	Lights
Makeup	Musical Instrument	Props
Publicity	Transportation	Usher
Set Construction	Sound	Special Effects
Anywhere you need me		

Child Photo Parental Release

Date _____

I, the undersigned parent or legal guardian of my son/daughter, do hereby give my authorization for the following waiver which is to apply to my son/daughter:
_____.

I hereby give _____, the director of _____, permission, including all rights of every kind and character whatsoever in and to all work done by me and poses, acts, plays, and appearances made by me for the videotape and/or program, as well as in and to the right to use my child's name and photographs, either still or moving, for commercial and advertising purposes in connection therewith. I further give said producers the right to reproduce in any manner whatsoever the recordings made by me hereunder of my child's voice and all instrumental, musical, or other sound effects produced by my child.

_____
(Signature of Parent/Guardian)

_____
(Printed Name)

Street Address:_____

City/State/Zip:_____

Phone:_____

Emergency Form

Authorization to consent to Emergency Medical Treatment

Student's Name:_____

Telephone numbers where parents can usually be reached in case of an emergency.

Mother's Name:_____

Phone(h):_____Phone(w):_____ (cell)_____

E-mail address: _____

Father's Name: _____

Phone(h):_____Phone(w):_____ (cell)_____

E-mail address: _____

Emergency contact if parent cannot be reached:

Name:_____ Relationship:_____ Phone: _____

Special medical consideration regarding my child: (examples: allergies to medicine or food, diabetes, etc.)

_____

Name of physician:_____

Phone: _____

Hospital preference: Nearest_____ Preferred _____

Insurance Provider _____ # _____

   I hereby authorize_____, through the adult person into whose care said child has been entrusted to consent to any emergency x-ray examination, anesthetic, medical or surgical diagnosis, treatment and/or hospital care for him/her, under supervision of and as deemed advisable by a physician licensed under the Medicine Practice Act. It is understood that this authority is given in advance of the need for any diagnosis, treatment, or medical care and is to provide authority to said adult person should the need arise. This authorization shall remain effective throughout each rehearsal, performance, or regular meeting during the current session, unless sooner revoked in writing and delivered to said adult person.

   I hereby agree to hold _____ and any volunteers, harmless from all liability which may arise as a result of my child's participation in the activities mentioned above. I understand that the activities involved in_____may involve risk or accidental injury and I hereby voluntarily assume such risk.

Signature_____Date_____
            (Parent or Guardian)

Emergency Protocol Guidelines

During any portion of the production process, the following guidelines should be considered.

Minor Injury or Illness

All injuries, regardless of how insignificant, must be made known to the Stage Manager or Director as soon as possible.

Standard first-aid procedures should be followed in each situation no matter how minor it may be.

If an injury is sustained which may require stitches, x-rays or other medical attention, then another adult person will assist the injured in getting the proper medical treatment.

If the injured person does leave the site for medical attention, ask him or her if anyone should be informed of the situation. Refer to that individual's Emergency Form for names and numbers.

Major Injury or Illness

Immediately upon the discovery of an injury or illness, the pre-designated persons are to be summoned to the scene to assess the situation and give directions for:

Attention to the injured party.

Contacting the emergency personnel: paramedic/fire/ambulance/police, etc.

Insuring that the cause of the present situation has been neutralized and is no longer a threat to others.

Contacting immediate family or friend of injured persons with:

- accurate and appropriate assessment of the situation
- destination, location, and approximate time of arrival to a medical facility
- appropriate volunteer(s) to transport the party(s) to the location where medical attention will be continued

Notify appropriate school personnel to attend to the needs on-site.

Fire: Make entire production staff, cast, and crew aware of alarm locations, fire extinguishers, and evacuation procedures. It is always a good idea to inform the fire department of the fire, even if it has been extinguished. When encountering more serious fires, contact the fire department immediately. Evacuate the building.

Theft: If a theft is discovered, contact the proper authorities and make any reports that may be required. If a theft is caught in the act, make everyone aware with as much noise as possible. Do not attempt to apprehend the thief. Surround yourself with others.

Assault: Any staff, cast, or crew who becomes the victim of an assault should contact the staff immediately. Any injuries should be assessed and tended to. Immediately contact the proper authorities. Investigate the circumstances of the assault and take the necessary steps to prevent future incidents.

Any Incident Involving a Minor

All incidents involving a child or minor will require you to follow the guidelines listed above in "Major Injury or Illness." In every case, the parent(s) or legal guardian(s) must be notified.

Suggested Performance Guidelines
for Cast and Crew

Before Performance

- Costumes must not be worn from home to school and vice versa.
- Upon arrival: check in with appropriate designated staff.
- Call time for all cast, choir, crew members, etc., is one hour prior to show time unless specified otherwise.
- Do not bring any food into the school, performance areas, or any dressing area.
- All on-stage props will be placed before the house opens.
- No member of the cast can be seen by an audience member while in costume.
- Please leave all items of value at home.

During Performance

- A call for "places" will be given five minutes prior to curtain.
- Regardless of the time, no member of the cast, crew, choir, orchestra, staff, etc., will begin the performance without the final word of the Stage Manager and/or Production Coordinator.
- Anyone who is not on-stage must remain in their proper waiting areas and out of the way of working cast and crew.
- Unless you are waiting for an entrance, never watch the performance from the wings.
- Never enter the audience in costume to watch the show from the back. *Never!*
- There is to be no unnecessary talking or other noise-making backstage.
- If the production is a period play, do not wear modern jewelry, watches, eyeglasses, etc., once in costume. It is a good practice to leave theme items at home.

Intermission

- During intermission do not socialize with any guests or other audience members. The performance is not over until the end of the show. Do not break the illusion of reality for the audience.
- Do not eat food while in costume and makeup.

After Performance

- Do not bring family members, friends, etc., to any backstage or dressing room areas. These areas are restricted and for cast and crew only.
- Costumes/props should be placed in prearranged places or hung neatly for the next performance.
- All personal items should be removed and taken home each night.
- Be aware that any comments you make aloud are easily overheard by others. Therefore, comments to audience members about the performance should be kept positive in nature as this is the time people look for reasons to accept or deny all that just took place on stage.

Community Emergency Telephone Numbers

Ambulance Co.: _____

Fire Department: _____

Police Department: _____

Sheriff Department: _____

Poison Control Center: _____

Hospital: _____

24 Hour Pharmacy: _____

Principal: _____

School Custodian: _____

Costume List

Line Number	Character Description	Character Name	Costume/ Shoes	Actor's Name Sizes	Borrowed From

General Prop List

Number	Item	Hand Held	Set Prop	Borrow	Name	Buy	Make

Makeup/Hair List

Line Number	Character Description	Actor	Makeup and Hair Description	Needed	Who is Doing

Ticket Checkout

Performance Date_____   Performance Time_____

Number	Given to / Phone #	How Many	Ticket Numbers	Date Paid / Date Returned	Total

Ticket Sales

Performance Date_____   Performance Time_____

Number	Sold to / Phone #	How Many	Cash / Check # Charge	Date Paid	Total

Lighting and Sound Cues

Page Number	The Cue / Dialogue	Character	Light Cue	Sound Cue	Notes

Chapter Eight

The Administrator

"Why are you deflating like a balloon?"

Once Upon a Time in Cindyland ...

And I woke up this morning, feeling so good. What did it matter that the rain was falling, the air so cold my breath was coming out in little puffy clouds? I was doing a great thing for my son. This week, Mr. Dennis was coming to Finn's classroom to write the lyrics to the song, we were starting blocking, and my son was actually ready for school on time. My life could not have been better.

With visions of my child bowing before a beaming audience — which somehow leads to him becoming president of the entire free world all because he got to do this performing arts program — I drop him off at the MPR. Our principal is there. She waves me over.

OK, if my life were a movie, this is where you'd hear that ominous music. You, as an audience, would shove another handful of popcorn in your mouth as you shake your head at how utterly clueless I am. I head over to the principal, expecting huge thanks for the great job I'm doing, or at worst to tell me she has to change the date of our performance.

Instead of showering me with gratitude, she tells me, "You've got to rewrite the play. I've had complaints from several parents." Like an anvil, my heart drops into my stomach. "Is this play appropriate for the kids?" she asks. My hackles rise. Isn't my son in the classroom? Is she accusing me of being an irresponsible parent? I wonder, but say nothing. She complains of the language, like the use of the words "stupid" and "incompetent." "And there's a queen? I just can't follow the story," she tells me.

Now mind you, she isn't doing this in the privacy of her office where I have a chance to justify my choices. She's doing this in the crowded MPR where every few seconds little Johnnie or sneezing Suzie are free to interrupt. So this conversation sounds more like: "I've had several complaints about the play from parents ... what, little Suzie? You lost a tooth? (back to me) I just don't think it's appropriate ... Oh, hi Johnnie, how's your mother?" I'm left standing there, with two or three complete omelets on my face, unable to defend myself coherently because children are interrupting, and she can't complete a sentence. I get my wits about me. After all, I'm not one of her employees. I'm a volunteer who has actually assisted in bringing several thousand dollars into this school. *And* I'm a mommy. In my brief moment of self-esteem, I tell her to call me.

As I walk back to the car, the rain has parted. The air has warmed, but I'm so angry I could spit bullets. Thoughts like "I quit," and "No good deed goes unpunished" tromp across my mind. I go home. My husband is actually angrier at my treatment than I am. He says, "Maybe Finn will be OK if you don't do this." And though every pore inside me is agreeing with my husband, there's my son's joy. I've got to suck this up for him.

How to Navigate the Challenges of Putting on a Program

In your world, the one holding you back may not be the administrator of your school. "She" could be one of the parents of the children, your husband or wife, or a concerned teacher or coworker. They are always armed with a politician's smile, a befuddled expression, and "the best of intentions." And they will most definitely cross your path. But they don't have to beat you down. There are ways to deal with them so you both feel better about yourselves.

Cindy's TLC Tip #876

Starbucks adds menu items based on the season. Odds are there's something you haven't tried. Now's the time. Go treat yourself to something caramely, or extra mochay. If it's hot out they may have something blendy and lemonadey. The point is you deserve the relaxing atmosphere and a treat. Besides, it's a well-known fact that stress burns calories, so you could have a Venti triple shot, five-pump-mocha and still be losing weight.

Taking Action

You are the hero of this piece, remember? Whether the really pretty princess or the handsome caped crusader, you will need to rise, scathed but stronger, to live to fight another battle for your child. There are some simple tools to help you go from feeling like a victim or ready to explode with anger to pretty darn near awesome. But you've got to do all the steps. Don't cheat and do just one. All of them!

You will need:

• Stickers

• Index cards

• Pretty rainbow colored pens

Step One — Support

I'll start. Wow. I want you to take a moment and notice all the great things you've done so far: you guided a passel of little people towards an experience they will treasure for the rest of their lives, you showed them that reading and writing is an awesome thing, you inspired them to want to learn more, and you gave them a reason to go to school. I say again, "Wow. Yay for you!"

As much as I'd like to think my words have an amazing power over you, I know they are not as powerful as what you say to yourself. So let's see if we can find a way for you to say some nice things to yourself and mean it! And we're going to do this in four easy steps.

Get out those stickers, index cards, and pretty rainbow colored pens. Or just index cards and a pen if stickers and pretty rainbow pens aren't your thing.

Make yourself a cup of tea or coffee. But please, put it in your favorite cup and saucer, or, the pretty flowered china that you only bring out for company, or your favorite mug you've had since college. Sit down at the table with your warm brew, your cards, your stickers, and pens. Take out one card and remember a compliment you've received for something you created. It can be the cherry pie or chili you made last week, the wall you painted in the family room, the cupboard you made or organized, or best yet, the compliment you received from your little guys when they said, "This play is funny." Any compliment will work.

Now, write down the compliment on the card. This isn't silly nonsense. Write it down! Even if you feel childish, write it down.

We need all the love and support the little ones do, sometimes more. It hurts when we've created this amazing parade and someone comes along and pees on it. Let's face it, if you're a parent and your child comes to you, her freckled face tear-stained, "Cloe says I'm ugly!" Are you going to say, "Well, Kara, empirically speaking, beauty is an arbitrary rating system created by ... ?" No! You're going to be a loving, supportive, and protective mommy or daddy and say something like, "Kara, you're beautiful and Cloe is a butthead." Kara will feel better and loved. You need to feel that way, too. Be that loving mommy or daddy to yourself. Even when you make a royal mistake, notice what you did right, realize that's one way not to do it, and move on.

If stickers and pretty rainbow pens are your thing, then it's time to decorate your card with those stickers and pretty pens. Yes, it may feel uncomfortable. Yes, it will feel childish. But isn't that strange that we can easily destroy the amazing things we do by dismissing them? Or we can beat ourselves up at the drop of a hat? Or we can stew for hours on one tiny thing someone said wrong about us, but we feel foolish or that we're wasting our time when we have to build ourselves up. Silly us.

Put one of the cards in your wallet. Good job! Yay for you! But you're not done yet.

Step Two — Regrouping

"I'm mad as hell and I'm not going to take it any more!"

— From the movie *Network*

Remember your other parent volunteers? It's time to rally them. You can call them, e-mail them, or send word via carrier owl. Sometimes it's easier to speak to them one at a time. Sometimes you feel better gathering them into a group. Do what's comfortable for you.

Tell the other parents about the conversation you've had with administrator or angry parent or coworker.

My personal saying, "Hell hath no fury like a volunteer scorned!"

These parents who have been in the trenches with you know what good you've done for their child. This program means something to them. They will rally on your behalf. Take heart, Little Phoenix, your broken heart will rise again and it will most likely be on the wings of these supportive volunteers.

Step Three — Receive

After you've told your story, take in every nice and supportive thing they say to you. *Do not* say, "You helped, too," or "It was nothing." Just listen and say, "Thank you." You can even respond with, "That means a lot." But that's it. Your job now is to feel better. Let them help you do that.

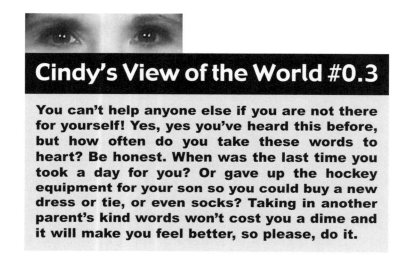

Cindy's View of the World #0.3

You can't help anyone else if you are not there for yourself! Yes, yes you've heard this before, but how often do you take these words to heart? Be honest. When was the last time you took a day for you? Or gave up the hockey equipment for your son so you could buy a new dress or tie, or even socks? Taking in another parent's kind words won't cost you a dime and it will make you feel better, so please, do it.

Step Four — Game Plan

It's now up to them to come up with a game plan, which they'll do. It will probably involve a meeting with the administrator, parent, coworker, or neighbor who is giving you all this grief. But if everyone keeps their head, you will all find there's a simple resolution to the problem.

It's all about me ... I mean you.

The best part of this for you, dear director, is that you don't have to do anything. They will rise to your defense. They will sing your praises. They will fight for this little play to continue. The hard part for you will be letting them do that. You're the kind of parent or teacher who cares and you want to help, I know, but this is not the time. You see, those other parent volunteers are invested now, too. They want this play to happen because their child is reading and liking it. Their child cares about going to school. Their child is most likely more articulate and happier than they've ever been before. Welcome to the magic of performing arts. And you made that happen.

Meanwhile, Back in Cindyland ...

So my story doesn't have a happy ending — yet.

As I finished off my second pint of Ben and Jerry, I began to understand why I was so upset. It wasn't the criticism, she's the principal — it's her job to look after the children. It was the way she said it. She clearly didn't know about the "Oreo Cookie Principle" of giving out her thoughts.

The Oreo Cookie Principle is how I was taught to give criticism. First say something you like about the person or the work they've done, then say what's bugging you, and then wrap up your point with a nicety. Since the OCP was named for the famous cookie, I figured everybody knew to use it. I was wrong.

The principal didn't have anything nice to say. And worst of all, she went for my jugular, my mommy gene, by insinuating that I was doing something inappropriate for the children. I felt shame. I felt like a bad parent.

What she didn't know is that I would retaliate by eating a vat of ice cream.

Since Ben and Jerry can enlighten the dimmest of beings, I saw that I had taken the first step towards self-doubt.

Cindy's View of the World #19

Self-doubt is an insidious monster. It looks like someone who has your best interests at heart. These well-meaning creatures don't want you to "make a mistake," or "get hurt," or "fail." In actuality, they've given up going after their dreams and artistic visions and the fact that you are makes them look at themselves. It's not a pleasant image so they'll shatter your mirror rather than face their own. Word of warning, once you begin that dead man's walk, it's hard to come back. Do not doubt yourself. You did an amazing thing. Always remember that. This would be a good time to get out that index card, don't you think? Actually, make a new one. Make ten. You're great because I said so and so does most everyone else.

Meanwhile, Back in Cindyland ... continued

Happily Ever After?

My group of parents did rally. They asked me to join them in their march into the administrator's office. She behaved as any good bureaucrat does. She backed down, eventually explaining, "It was actually just one parent and she wasn't really so much upset as concerned ... *but* other parents could be. So be careful." Wow, talk about your inspiring speech. Made me want to run out there and ... eat more ice cream.

The other parents were pleased with the results. They got what they wanted. The program would go on. Their child would be served. But sadly, my inner child was still feeling hungry. The parade I was hoping for just wasn't going to happen.

I left her office searching for more than anything Ben and Jerry could offer. Ironically, I found what I needed — the parade. It just wasn't from the administrator.

It was in the parents who had "marched" into her office in my defense. It was in the voices of my husband and friends who shouted outrage. It was in the faces of the children who beamed when I said, "I'm here to teach acting today."

I think it's time for me to get out an index card, don't you?

Cindy's TLC Tip #976

Put on Gloria Gaynor's *I Will Survive*. Oh, silly you, crank it up, like you use to when you were sixteen and alone with your parents' stereo. Now sing! At the top of your lungs, "I will survive!" For those of you who prefer the rock band approach, dust off your air guitars and pull out those number two pencils to play the drum solo of your favorite rock song. Play along the whole time. You deserve it. You totally rock.

Chapter Nine

Running Through the Show

"What's my line again?"

Knee deep in the show and you're probably starting to wonder if this was a good idea. You were busy before, right? But now it's beginning to feel like you've fallen victim to ... *The Show That Ate Your Life* . Aaaach! Everyone is after you: the kids with their endless questions, the crew with their endless questions, and the administration with their endless questions. It's enough to make a poor hapless hero want to give in. Ah, but you are Super Director, you can slay small costume problems with a single thought, run-through faster than a speeding bullet, and make it home in time for dinner with your family.

Take Care of You

"To keep the body in good health is a duty ... Otherwise we shall not be able to keep our mind strong and clear."

— Buddha

Munching

I know, I sound like your mother here, but are you eating right? Silly as it seems, make sure you're getting enough protein and sleep. We tend to run to carbs when the stress hits the fan, and that's OK, just keep that food balance in your life. Toss in a bit of fish or a smitch of chicken on that cracker.

Cindy's TLC Tip #9

Don't waste precious time just sitting at a traffic light. Take a nap. The blaring of all those car horns could "caress" you back to wakefulness.

Movement

Are you making time to go for a short walk or a swim? Nothing clears the cobwebs like a bit of exercise. No, I'm not saying you need to run the marathon. But whenever I'm in the midst of a show and ideas and people are coming at me full throttle, I find getting out and getting a bit of activity calms me down. So how about today you park a little further away and walk those extra steps to the store or work? Maybe you take the stairs instead of the elevator. Did you know it is one stair per calorie? It's true.

Mood

"Here in this body are the sacred rivers: here are the sun and moon as well as the pilgrimage places ... I have not encountered another temple as blissful as my own body."

— Saraha

Please, dear hero, be like Saraha and cherish *you*. Treat yourself to a nice thing. Maybe it's a new pen for the show. Or, how about buying a gooshy pair of socks? Don't spend a lot of money, but don't be chintzy, either. You can't take care of everyone else if you're not OK.

Take Care of the Show

"Even cowards can endure hardship; only the brave can endure suspense."

— Mignon McLaughlin

With your spirit and body intact, it's time to tackle the show. You are going to start doing run-throughs. This is exactly like it sounds. You run-through any portion of the show. Start with scenes you've blocked, then begin putting the scenes together until you're running the whole show. Run-throughs give the actors a sense of continuity and rhythm.

In addition to doing run-throughs, there are other simple, easy things you can do to get your play in fighting shape.

Notes

After your actors finish a run-through of a scene, an act, or the whole play, depending on how far along you are, it's important to give them feedback. This is called *notes*.

What follows are some simple and easy rules.

Say Something to Everyone

No matter the size of the role, take a moment and notice what a good job each person is doing. "Suzy, that was wonderful nose-picking, honey." Whatever it is. This way, everyone feels important. If you can't get to little Johnnie today, make sure you get to him sometime soon.

Encourage a Performance

If your actor guys are not doing what you want, but they're close, say, "I really liked when you stood on your head, now could you do that for a little longer?" If they just aren't understanding what you're asking them to do and you've asked several times, you have a couple of choices: you could belabor the point until you want to pull your hair out, or you could let it go and focus on another actor who is a bit stronger and work with them.

Be Kind

Be as kind as humanly possible, without lying. We all know when someone isn't telling the truth, particularly kids. There's no easier way to lose their trust than to tell them something that isn't true.

Avoid Giving Line Readings

Remember our James Earl Jones story? Don't tell an actor, "Say it like this." For so many reasons: it's considered insulting, what if you think you're giving the line reading of your life and you're not, and actors, no matter the age, need to find the character in themselves, not in you.

Be Firm

You are the captain of this ship and you don't want a mutiny on your hands. So if you're asked, "Why?" Give an answer, even if it's the wrong one. Or better yet, "I'll get back to you," if you don't know. And whatever you do, get back to them, even if it's to say, "I'm still noodling on that."

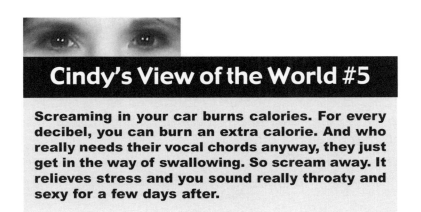

Cindy's View of the World #5

Screaming in your car burns calories. For every decibel, you can burn an extra calorie. And who really needs their vocal chords anyway, they just get in the way of swallowing. So scream away. It relieves stress and you sound really throaty and sexy for a few days after.

Pacing

Actors tend to like to take very long pauses in between their lines. I think they think it makes them seem like they're thinking deep thoughts. In reality, it makes them look slow and makes the play drag on forever. So get them to pick up the pace between their lines. They can take as long as they need while they're giving the lines, but when you're able to drive a Mack truck through their pauses, it's gone on too long.

Blocking Tips

Use these tips in your show and your kids will actually look like little professionals.

Scene/Not a Scene

What is it about little guy productions, and I'm talking right on through high school, where the kids stand eighty feet apart? As an audience, you see that and you're not sure where to look. So I have created a system to help the kids remember. It's called Scene/Not a Scene. When they are standing in somewhat close proximity, I call that a scene. When they are standing in two separate continents, I call that not a scene. The goal is to make them be in as many "scenes" as possible. Scene/Not a Scene helps make your show look tight.

Planting Feet

The other curse of the young actor is shifting feet. They squirm more than a cat that doesn't want to be hugged. They must plant their feet, which means don't move them. Pretend the feet are glued to the floor, unless the actor is crossing the stage or dancing. That's it!

Projection

You've spent countless hours working on the show, yet you can't hear a word because the little darlings are mumbling worse than Marlon Brando at the dentist. They need to speak up. One great exercise my friend and acting coach, Cliff Weissman, uses is have the kids practice speaking like they do on the playground, their outdoor voice, then say their line from the play.

Rehearse

Practice, practice, practice as much and as often as you can. There is nothing better for a show than rehearsal. I usually figure one hour per page minimum for just running through the show.

Along with that, get them off-book as soon as possible. This frees them to remember all the other things you'll want them to do, like walk and talk at the same time.

A Stop and Start

These are run-throughs that you stop and start again. You do this to go over a moment or a beat that the actor has missed — repeatedly. By stopping when the problem arises, the actor has a chance to do it again and finally get it right. What often happens is that your little star does it exactly like you want it. Then you run the scene and they forget it all. So you stop and start the scene again.

Word of warning here: Keep in mind the big picture. You have limited amount of time and lots to do. Don't sacrifice the many for the good of the one moment. Good rule of thumb: If your actor doesn't get it in the fourth or fifth try, move on. They may just need some gestation time.

Treats

Remember, we're all kids, so just say yes to cookies, protein bars, or whatever makes you feel happy. If a mom wants to bring in brownies, let her. But just make sure to give them to the kids at the end of the rehearsal, or they'll have such a sugar rush you'll be doing your play on the ceiling. Unless, of course, you want to pick up the pace, then there's no better way than a hunk of chocolate cake.

Taking Care of the Crew

"The idea of strictly minding our own business is moldy rubbish. Who could be so selfish?"

— Myrtle Barker

It's time to check-in and make sure things are moving along. Props, costumes, and ticket sales all should be happening. Translation is: You need to be seeing some props and costumes coming in, and tickets need to be sold. Don't wait until the last minute.

Something fun for everyone is to have a contest to see who sells the most tickets, or who sells the first ten tickets. You can chart it on poster board. Maybe even set a goal of X amount of tickets by X date and graph how close the company is coming. The prizes don't have to be much. This might be a good time to give away that horrible clown statue you got at your wedding. Oh, I'm kidding. Treats, toys from the dollar store, or a gift card is all you need to keep everyone happy.

Remember to say "please," "thank you," and "help!"

Cindy's TLC Tip #54

Go out and get a cheap-o calendar and some stick-on-stars, you can probably get this at the ninety-nine cent store, on sale even. Now every time you do a good job, mark it in the calendar with one of your stars. It's OK if you have so many stars on one day you can't see the date. Try not to let a day go by without putting on at least one star. After all, "We are such stuff as dreams are made of."

 **Chapter Ten**

Final Dress

"I think I'm gonna throw up!"

Yippee! Yahoo! You did it! You survived run-through ... only to be thrown into "hell week" (Ominous music — dum de dum dum). You are about to enter the Dress Rehearsal Zone. That final week when everything falls apart, when you think only disaster can come from such madness, when you're so stressed you've gone beyond what could even vaguely resemble a diet. But take heart, for it will come together.

It's time for an anecdote or twelve.

Once Upon a Time in Cindyland ...

We were doing our play *Wild Dust*, you remember, the one we wrote in a week? Well, it was final dress. And up to that point, everything that could go wrong had gone wrong and was getting wronger, so we were due for some good luck, right? Wrong again.

The girl playing Belle had a panic attack, brought on by acute anxiety, and started throwing up in what could be loosely called our dressing room — it was actually the girl's bathroom of a MPR. So we had no Belle. And I, the director, who was also playing the blind woman because the original actress had dropped out just four or five days before, said to the cast, "The show must go on." They rallied, as all good casts do, around the girl playing Belle. Two of the actors refused to go on. Instead, they opted to comfort the girl who wasn't really sick. So we were now three women down out of a ten-person play. I went on with the final dress. But I lost another actress because she couldn't handle the pressure. She disappeared into the boy's bathroom to cry her eyes out in large gut-wrenching sobs. I know you think I'm making this up, but I'm not.

Once Upon a Time in Cindyland ... continued

On the dress went with me now not only playing the blind woman, but the two other women who had rallied around Belle. Now mind you, I didn't really know my lines. So before I spoke every line I said a silent prayer, "Please let me remember what I'm suppose to say." Flip, who was playing the only male in the show, a cowboy named Cooper, took over the part of the sobbing woman. It was the most horrific dress rehearsal I had ever been through up to that point. I now have been through a few worse, or almost as bad. We came into opening night sure we had a disaster on our hands. But here's the thing, we didn't. It was like the Theatre God had taken pity on us and opening night rocked. The show came together by magic. Or blood. Or force of will. I'm not sure. But it came together. And your show will, too.

Want another story? Hush, of course you do.

We were doing the *Queen's New Heater*, my son's third grade show. It was the day before we were supposed to open. The kids did not know their lines or their blocking. And I had a 103 degree fever. Flip had just been diagnosed with stage 3+ cancer of the colon. I even had one of the parents assisting me say, "The kids cannot cognitively get this. They're just not ready." This was right before the last hour of our final dress. I was beside myself. Visions of my son's humiliation danced through my head. I was devastated. This thing I had taken on to make my son's life better, this gift I wanted to give him, to thank him for all the years he'd schlepped from one camp to the next, was deteriorating before my eyes. And I could see the principal's smug face as she knowingly nodded.

Disaster, right? Wrong. I don't know how those little ones pulled it out. Maybe it was our sheer determination, but they came together in a way I cannot even begin to explain. I don't think I've ever been prouder of a company in my whole life. They got up on that stage and by the grace of whatever power you believe in, they knew their lines, their blocking, they were loud, and they actually got laughs. Laughs! There is an even better happy ending for this story. But I'm not going to share that with you quite yet. Read on, my lovely, and believe.

"For there are more things in heaven and earth that are dreamed of in your philosophy." *

Hell Week

This is when you're going to pull all the pieces together. But first you've got to find out what your pieces are.

Working with the Actors

If you're working with kids over eleven, it's time for the *shotgun* — a fast-paced talk-through of the play. Flip and I like to call it Ipecac for the show because it gets rid of any of the icky pauses and tired line readings. What you do is get your actors up on their feet and have them start pacing back and forth. Then, have your actors say their lines as quickly as possible. The trick to a good shotgun is that you make sure there are no pauses between the lines. None. Zip. Nada. You listen intently and if you hear a pause, you make them do the line again and again until it's gone. I have seen professional actors brought to their knees because they were so intimidated by the shotgun. But I've got to tell you, if you want to have your show move and have energy, this is the way to do it.

If your kids are under eleven, this is way too much for them. Apply the same idea, but make them go through the lines of the show quickly with no pacing. Don't make them repeat over and over, once or twice is good.

Working with the Costumes

It's time for little children to stumble, saunter, and flit across your vision dressed in their merry little costumes. The *costume parade* is to be done at the beginning of Hell Week, because you are about to find out that the green you thought would look good on the skinny red head kid actually makes him look like a damaged broccoli and the princess dress you thought would look so sweet is actually two sizes too small and you'll have to completely rethink the costume. Your designer will run out of the theatre screaming ... not really, just sort of shouting.

The designer will make notes on the trusty form you had given him or her weeks ago and go to a thrift store, where you will go over budget, but you don't care because it's for the kids.

As soon as any child has a costume that makes you happy, let them work in it. But be careful because they love to drink grape juice or anything else that can stain during this week.

Working with the Set

Up until now you've probably been working with replacement parts to your set: a folding chair is your throne and the backdrop from the winter carnival is your flats. Not any more. As soon as that set is ready, it's time for the little ones to clamber up on top and start running the show.

Be careful though, because this is when you find out about all the nails that weren't nailed down, all the steps that weren't sanded, and the doors that weren't put on right. And all of them will need to be fixed.

In addition, you actually now get to see that the way you've blocked the show, with the set in mind, is totally wrong. You either didn't plan enough space or too little, so your actors are shoved together like sardines while the rest of the stage is completely empty. You will need to re-block here, or you can leave it as is and explain in your curtain speech that you're doing the Avant-garde, non-linear version of *Jack and Jill.*

Working with the Props

It's time to give the "if it's not yours, don't touch" speech, about a hundred million times. To excited little people the props can become the most magical things: a pencil can become a knife to poke and prod someone's eye out, a ball can become a ... ball, and a cup can become a crown to shove onto another actor's head who doesn't really want it and will start to cry and whine until a fight breaks out. So give the speech. Say it with me. "If it's not yours, don't touch it." And then offer up some consequences for their actions, which you probably won't stand by anyway. It's OK. Trust me. You're doing well.

Props should now be on the carefully labeled prop table and no child should be swarming around. If the prop is not their prop, they don't touch it. Say it loud and proud. "If it's not yours, don't touch it." Good, you've said it three times. Only ninety-nine million plus to go.

Working with the Lights

This particular rehearsal is called a *cue-to-cue.* What that means is a few of your more trustworthy actors, and their parents, stand On-stage while the lighting and sound team gets a chance to run-through the lights and sound. It's called a cue-to-cue because you don't go through the whole script, just the cues. If there are four pages of dialogue between one lighting cue and the next, skip those four pages. It should go without saying, the same holds true for sound cues, but just thought I'd say it.

If you don't have lights and sound, smart you! But then again, you don't get the joy of finding out that what you just re-blocked is actually worse than the blocking you had before, because there's no lights that hit that spot. Time to block, again! Or you don't get to discover that the mics only pick up the section right around the actor speaking and nothing else. More blocking. You aren't going to experience the surprise that the cue you taped to sound like a waterfall actually sounds like a toilet flushing.

The trick to surviving your cue-to-cue is to stay fluid. Some things are not going to go the way you like, but most will.

Cindy's TLC Tip #33

If thou art a maiden, get thee to an ice creamery.

If thou art a dude, you're off to Home Depot. And this is just for you. No "honey-do list," no broken gutters to fix. This is your time! All I can say, buddy, is you're free. No guilt, no doubt. Try out every power tool. Wander the aisles until they kick you out. Make a wish list of everything you'd buy if you won the lottery. Dream big. Dreams are free. This is a gimme.

Working with the Party

Every show needs to have a cast party. It's a celebration of all you've accomplished. And the kids really treasure it. If you haven't already started planning your party, now is the time.

You can have your soirée either after opening night or after closing night. Ask a parent volunteer to coordinate it. It can be a potluck or everyone can chip in a small amount of money and you can order food. You'll need a place to have it. An empty classroom, a cast member's home, or a park are all good places. Have plenty of room for the kids to run free. It's nice if you can give some kind of certificate, or something, to "honor" the little people.

Final Dress

"Can't forget, can't regret, what I did for love." * *

I believe the adage, "Bad final dress, great opening night," was a big fat rationalization created so hapless directors wouldn't run from the theatre screaming, "It's gonna be a disaster."

All the pieces are now pulled together in a final run-through, or seven, depending on how late you are allowed to keep the little ones. Costumes, props, makeup, lights, and sound, it's all up on the stage at one time, you hope.

If you have time to give notes, keep them incredibly positive. Your actors and crew have worked hard and they need all the love and support you can give them.

Now go home and get some rest. You want to look rested for your big opening night.

Cindy's TLC Tip #A25

Take a luxurious bath. Light some candles, bring in the boom box with a CD of your favorite Gershwin tunes, use the bubbles that are only there for company, and climb in. Savor the warmth. Let the water ease your tired muscles and your weary heart.

If hot baths aren't your thing, you so need a mini-vacation. But sadly, escaping to a desert isle just can't happen — for several more weeks — because the little people are counting on you. Instead, how about taking a trip to the local game store: Best Buy, or Game Stop. Give yourself at least an hour. And do this alone. So there's nobody standing by whining, "Can we go now?" Now let loose. I want you to sit in front of the big screen TV and watch. Oh, but you are so not done. Time to head over to the stereophonic section; you get to try out every single speaker system they have. Pretend the thrum of the music drowning out your voice is the beat of the local island drums. Oh wait, there's more. Go to the game section. Have you played the new Wii? Xbox? Try them all out. Wasn't that just like a vacation? OK, not really, but at least you had time for you.

Now take a moment and look back on the last several weeks. Do you realize all you've done? How brave you were? Wow. (Applause.) That parenthetical is all the drama teachers, directors, actors, and parents that have come before you and did what you are about to do. Go to bed. Sleep the sleep of the deserving.

Trivia Time

*"More things under heaven and earth ... " The Bard strikes again. This quote is from his play, *Hamlet*. Hamlet is having an argument with his father's ghost — go figure.

* *"Can't forget, can't regret ... " From *A Chorus Line*, which is my all time favorite musical. It's the story of a bunch of chorus "kids" at an audition. First done in the 1970s, it was an unprecedented hit that actually went on to win a Pulitzer Prize.

Chapter Eleven

Opening Night

"I did it!"

Everyone's excited, scared, and anxious. As leader of this motley crew, you must keep everyone focused. But before we **"raise the curtain on the tragedy that has befallen the Bard's greatest comedy,"** * you're going to need to see to a few final details.

To Curtain Speech or Not to Curtain Speech

When the director gets up On-stage, before the show begins, and tells the audience about the work of the kids or to turn off their cell phones, this is the *curtain speech.* You can either give one or not. I do. My argument for it: rally the audience to your side. Ask them to be nice, to applaud, and to laugh, without actually saying it.

Cindy's Curtain Speech

"Hi. Hi! Hi! We're so glad you're here. And we're thrilled to be presenting (name of show). I just want to tell you a little about what you're about to see. [X] amount of weeks ago, this amazing group of young people came together. They wanted to put on a show. But more than that, they wanted to write it. Take it from page to stage. And that's what they did. From soup to nuts, everything you are about to see is theirs. They've been working before, during, and after class. They've volunteered to give up recess and stay after school. They've worked so incredibly hard and I'm really proud of them. I hope you are, too. Enjoy. Bye!"

You can use my curtain speech. You can modify it. You can do your own. Or you can not do one. The choice is totally up to you. Just remember, your excitement for the show will rub off on the audience.

Getting the Kids in Character

There is no worse sin in theatre than to break character. Oh my gosh, the skies open up, **"Fire and brimstone coming down ... rivers and seas boiling ... human sacrifice. Dogs and cats living together. Mass hysteria!"** * * OK, that's not really what happens, but it's bad. So you have to keep those little ones from breaking character.

Staying In Character

Where does the character begin? Off-stage. When does the character end? After the show. Say this to them about a bazillion times. Make the kids repeat it back to you during notes. Drill it into their minds. Remind them that they are creating a world for this audience, a magical place, and to break character is to shatter that world. It would be like Harry Potter saying, "There is no magic, I made up this whole story."

But it's not enough to tell them this. You have to show them how to make it happen.

The Character Game

With this game, some of the kids will fight you. The older they are, the more they think they know, the smarter they think they are, and the less they think they need this. Ha! Ignore them and insist they play. But you must play, too!

Once a child gets into their costume, they must walk and talk and behave like their character. They have to interact with the other kids as their character. They must enter the world of the play *and not leave* until the show is over.

Since you don't technically have a character, you can play the Queen, the Principal, or the Storyteller. Be whoever you wish to be. And abide by the rules you have set down for the kids: stay in character, no hitting, shoving, or body contact, even if your character would do that.

This game may feel goofy, but stick with it. The reward is tremendous.

Cindy's TLC Tip #13

It just doesn't seem fair that after all the work you've put in, you don't get to wear a costume. It's so much fun to dress up, isn't it? Of course it is. And the kids love it because you become part of their world. So go out and get yourself a costume piece that goes along with the show. If it's a fairy tale, don a tiara and that dress you bought for your cousin's wedding that you love but never get to wear or wear a crown and a sword in your belt loop. If it's a Western, get yourself those really cute, red cowboy boots you've always wanted or buy a lasso and try it out on your best friend. Treat yourself to one item that you can wear that symbolizes the show. And wear it!

Hold for Laughs

You've so belabored cue pick-up, by now your little darlings are probably running through the show at lightning speed. This is good. You'll have a fast-paced show the audience will enjoy.

However, the kids might barrel right on over the audiences' laughter. This is not good. We want the audience to laugh. We like laughter. Laughter is our friend and our goal. So, the kids must be reminded to hold. But not wait, there's a difference. *Waiting* will slow your production down, *holding* catches the audience long enough for them to chortle and move on.

How to hold for laughter? You have to listen to your audience. Laughter is like a wave, rising, peaking, and then rolling down. When the laughter is rising and peaking, the actor waits. As it starts to roll down, the actor resumes the show. This may be too advanced for the little people to get. But it will give them an image to hang on to. In the end, they will have to feel their way through.

"Now get out there, team" Speech

Before your actors go on, you want to get their energy up, so it's your time to give them "the speech." Think of yourself as a coach in one of those football movies, you are inspiring your team to play the best darn game of their lives. Use any tool at your disposal. It's OK to jump around, be silly, laugh, or cry. Whatever they need to realize that this is it. This is not a dress rehearsal, and if they don't bring it on now, then when? They don't want to wake up when this is over and feel like they woulda, coulda, shoulda. Today, right now, this performance is it! And they need to give it everything they have!

You get the picture?

Cindy's View of the World #5C

I believe that, as artists, we are here to "serve" the audience. Our goal is to entertain or enlighten them. And I want the kids to understand that what they're doing is about so much more than just *them*. Putting on this show, showing a painting, playing piano at a recital, they're making the world a better place through their creativity. But how do you show that? I ask each child to pick someone in the audience and do their performance for that person. It can be grandma, who has driven two hours to see them, mom, or their best friend. By giving their performance for that special person, suddenly kids who have refused to speak up, will be loud enough to rattle the roof. Children who couldn't focus are laser-sharp. In the end, somewhere down the road, these kids realize that what they do, how they act, matters. They can make a difference.

See to Any and All Last Minute Details

Double check that the props are where they're supposed to be, or check with your crew chief. Is your crew ready? Is every kid ready? Break a leg 'cause its time to ...

Open the Curtain

As director, you can stay backstage and help "run" the show, sit in the audience, or leave and get a very large drink — it's up to your imagination and budget. Your job is done. You are not needed anymore. It's totally up to you how you choose to handle yourself now.

Cindy's View of the World #58

I stick with the show right up to the bitter end. But I can't sit in the audience. It's completely nerve-wracking. I worry that the audience is not laughing, I worry that they are laughing. It's horrible. So I work backstage, driving the kids crazy, making sure they're staying in character, and ready to go on. This way I feel like I'm really in the trenches with them. We sink or swim together and I have the added bonus of not being bald when the show is over. My hands were too busy pulling curtains, running sets, and hugging children.

It's a Wrap

Practice saying, "Thank you," "Really? I'm glad you liked it. Thank you." You will want to apologize for every mishap and explain everything that should have gone right. Don't. Your line now is "Thank you." And if you start saying it now, maybe you'll actually do it when the time comes.

Trivia Time

* **"Raise the curtain on the tragedy ... "** is said by Martin Short in the movie *Get Over It*. This movie is a total delight. It's an updated spin on Shakespeare's *A Midsummer Night's Dream*. Don't miss it.

** **"Fire and Brimstone..."** Bill Murray says this to the Mayor in the original *Ghostbusters*. This is a great flick to watch around Halloween. Just save it for the eight and over set.

Chapter Twelve

It's Time to Celebrate

"You're the coolest person in the whole world!"

"Whenever I have to choose between two evils, I always like to try the one I haven't tried before."

— Mae West

Wow, can you hear that applause? That's for you and your kids. Let it fill you. Let the light from their faces warm your heart. You did it. Oh mighty director, you took those kids from page to stage. It's time to celebrate, just as soon as we get the strike done.

The Strike

The *strike* is another word for the cleanup. Everyone will pitch in and return the theatre space to its original beauty, before the sets and costumes and kids made a mess.

Everybody, including the little people, participate in this. It's particularly important for the children because they need to respect property that is not theirs. This also helps to build great habits for when they're at home. The community then looks to your kids positively and this will come in handy should you decide to do another production and/or want to increase your budget next year. And most important, though, is that it builds self-respect; the kids realize that they have the power to make a difference in the community they work in.

The Strike Planner

This handy dandy little Strike Planner form on page 120 helps you to organize your strike if you're the kind of person who likes to cross all your t's and dot all your i's. If you're a bit more casual, you can just make it a free-for-all; let everyone chip in and then you double-check everything when the strike is finished. Both can work; it's up to you.

Strike Must Dos

Make sure these three things are always done.

Everyone who donated something gets it back in the same condition, or better, than when they donated. This might mean you have to send an item or two to the cleaners. Or launder some things.

The theatre stage and seating area are swept and/or vacuumed. Every piece of paper is picked up and thrown away.

Bathrooms are left clean. No leftover makeup junk or hairpins hanging out on the bathroom counters. If everyone has left and something is left unclaimed, you have three choices: toss it, keep it, donate it, but do not leave it.

Reading the Form

It's pretty self-explanatory. There's a column for each department and then rows to determine what items need handling and who is handling the return. Meet with your crew heads or dedicated volunteers prior to beginning the strike. Plan, discuss, and then away you go.

Party on, Dude

Woo-hoo! You're done. The theatre is shiny as a bright new copper penny, so it's time for your cast party. Yikes, it may seem like a director's job is never done, but there are a few things you have to do at your soirée.

Acknowledge Your Crew

You can do a way cool speech about how you couldn't have done this without them, which you couldn't. Say each name and have them acknowledged with applause. You can hand out cards, gifts, gift cards, or flowers and say your thank you, again, giving each person a moment to stand and receive some heartfelt claps. Have them stand up, get some applause, and saying a nice word or two is good. Anything extra depends on your budget and time.

Acknowledge Your Actors

You want to thank all the little people ... literally. Give them a token of your appreciation, a certificate with their name on it. Have them march up and receive it while you hum "Pomp and Circumstance." Or you could give them a picture frame with a picture of the entire cast. They also like a toy that symbolizes the show. Make sure each child gets to come up and get something while thunderous applause fills their ears.

Acknowledge You

"Be really whole and all things will come to you."

— Lao Tzu

Odds are you won't get up and say, "Wow, I did an amazing job. I rock." Odds are that you will shyly accept the many compliments coming your way. You'll pass off the credit to the kids or to the mommies and daddies. And so that is why I have prepared this little gift for you, your very own paper crown on page 121.

Cindy's TLC Tip #X

At the party, have everyone autograph the back of your crown. Then, when you get home and you're feeling that tiny bit of letdown that it's all over, read those signatures. Take in everything that was written. Now decorate your crown. Make sure to put one gold star on it, that one is from me. You don't have to wear your crown, though I applaud you if you do. You can find a frame for it and hang it up for all to admire. You can put it up on your fridge. You can do just about anything with it as long as you leave it out for at least a week.

Eat, Drink, and Be Merry

"No trumpets sound when the important decisions of your life are made. Destiny is made known silently."

— Agnes De Mille

Your work is done. It's time now to celebrate. Eat up, oh heroic director, replenish and enjoy. You did it!

Cindy's View of the World #100

The year that Babe Ruth got the most strikeouts was the same year he got the most home runs. You will know doubt and uncertainty down this road, dear director. It's lonely being a dreamer. And it's so easy to get lost. A lot of people are more than happy to give you direction, which is usually wrong. When you find yourself wandering aimlessly, filled with doubt, remember, "This, too, shall pass." Just keep walking, you will see things come down a different way. Your dreams can come true if you believe ...

Once Upon a Time in Cindyland ...

A little thought for food.

Do you remember way back when we started this journey? When I started, my heart was thumping. I was terrified of failure, of success, of disappointing my son.

Well, I completed *The Queen's New Heater* in March of 2008, and my son still says that performing the show for the school was the most fun he's ever had. Isn't that cool?

But wait, there's more ... My happy ending I made you wait for.

The administrator who had made my journey so challenging came up to me after the show and apologized. She said she was wrong. She was glad I didn't listen to her. In fact, she had some sort of school district mucky-muck there to watch the show and he asked if my son's ordinary third grade class were in the fourth grade gifted program. I could have popped a button off the vest I was wearing right there. I was so proud.

And one last final piece

The other parents who came to see this little group of the third-graders-who-could invited me and my assistant, Annie, back next year. The school foundation wanted to hire us to put this program on for the whole school. Wow. Money and doing something I love that has meaning — could it get any better than this?

Once Upon a Time in Yourland ...

Hmmmm, I wonder what your story will be? Will it be that you conquer your fear of heights, lose that extra ten pounds, or maybe do this all again next year? The world is your oyster, baby. Nothing can stop you now!

"Oh the places you'll go."
— Dr. Seuss

Strike Planner

Production Title_____   Date_____

Department	Props	Costumes	Set Pieces	Makeup	Audio/Visual	Other
Item Who Returned						
Item Who Returned						
Item Who Returned						
Item Who Returned						
Item Who Returned						
Item Who Returned						
Item Who Returned						
Item Who Returned						
Item Who Returned						
Item Who Returned						

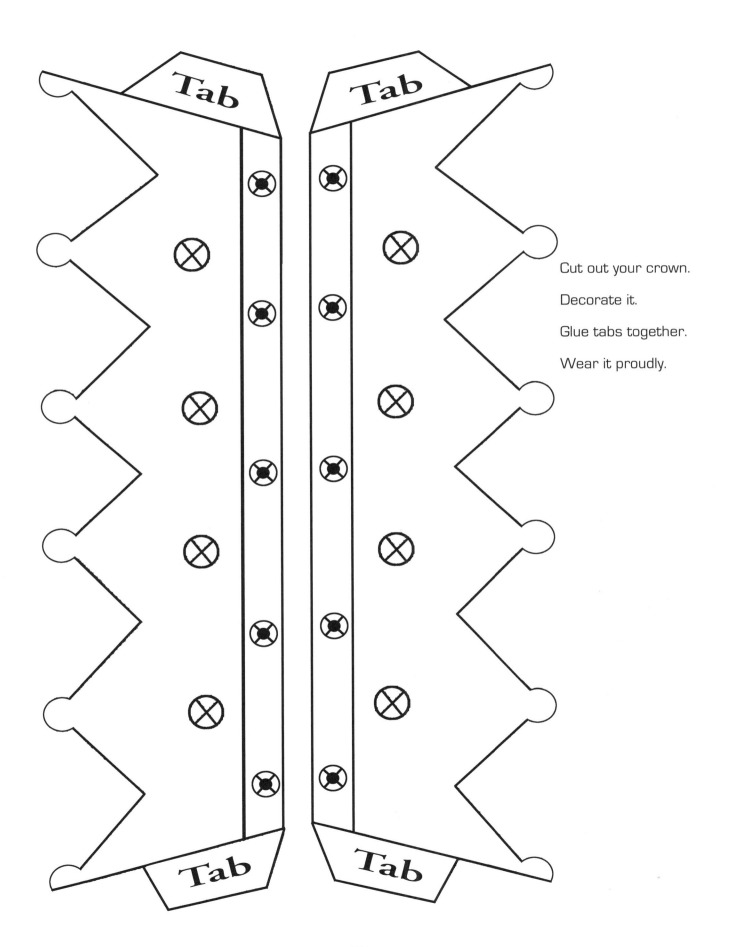

Cut out your crown.

Decorate it.

Glue tabs together.

Wear it proudly.

About the Author

Every year the staff of the Teenage Drama Workshop, a teen drama camp with classes and productions, chooses a student who best exemplifies what the program is all about. When Cindy was a teenager, she won an acting scholarship to the Workshop in Los Angeles. She's made her living in show business ever since. With her husband and writing partner Flip Kobler, she spent many years at Disney writing the sequels to *Lion King, Beauty and the Beast, Pocahontas, Lady and the Tramp, Hunchback of Notre Dame* and many, many others. She is now the front man for Showdown (www.showdownstageco.com), sharing her unique experience in Hollywood and passion for theatre with a new generation. Showdown is a national teen theatre program, taking teens from insecure and uncertain to empowered and employable. Showdown believes the arts can change young lives for the better. As an in-demand acting coach, she helps craft young actors and as a mentor, she supports young souls. As a writer, she continues to have plays published and screenplays sold, but working with young people is her true calling.

Order Form

Meriwether Publishing Ltd.
PO Box 7710
Colorado Springs CO 80933-7710
Phone: 800-937-5297 Fax: 719-594-9916
Website: www.meriwether.com

Please send me the following books and DVDs:

_____ **PLAYdate #BK-B307**   **$19.95**
by Cindy Marcus
A parent's and teacher's guide to putting on a play

_____ **Let's Put on a Show! #BK-B231**   **$19.95**
by Adrea Gibbs
A beginner's theatre handbook for young actors

_____ **Introduction to Theatre Arts —**   **$23.95**
Student Handbook #BK-B264
by Suzi Zimmerman
A 36-week action handbook for theatre arts instruction

_____ **Introduction to Theatre Arts —**   **$29.95**
Teacher's Guide #BK-B265
by Suzi Zimmerman
Teacher's Guide to Introduction to Theatre Arts

_____ **Everything About Theatre #BK-B200**   **$19.95**
by Robert L. Lee
The guidebook of theatre fundamentals

_____ **Theatre Games for Young Performers**   **$17.95**
#BK-B188
by Maria C. Novelly
Improvisations and exercises for developing acting skills

_____ **Getting Your Kicks! (DVD with workbook)**   **$34.95**
#BK-DV06
A beginner's guide to choreography

These and other fine Meriwether Publishing books are available at your
local bookstore or direct from the publisher. Prices subject to change
without notice. Check our website or call for current prices.

Name: _____ e-mail: _____

Organization name: _____

Address: _____

City: _____ State: _____

Zip: _____ Phone: _____

❏ **Check enclosed**
❏ **Visa / MasterCard / Discover / Am. Express #** _____

Signature: _____ *Expiration
date:* _____ / _____
(required for credit card orders)

Colorado residents: Please add 3% sales tax.
Shipping: Include $3.95 for the first book/DVD and 75¢ for each additional book/DVD ordered.

❏ *Please send me a copy of your complete catalog of books and plays.*

Order Form

Meriwether Publishing Ltd.
PO Box 7710
Colorado Springs CO 80933-7710
Phone: 800-937-5297 Fax: 719-594-9916
Website: www.meriwether.com

Please send me the following books and DVDs:

_____ **PLAYdate #BK-B307**   **$19.95**
by Cindy Marcus
A parent's and teacher's guide to putting on a play

_____ **Let's Put on a Show! #BK-B231**   **$19.95**
by Adrea Gibbs
A beginner's theatre handbook for young actors

_____ **Introduction to Theatre Arts —**   **$23.95**
Student Handbook #BK-B264
by Suzi Zimmerman
A 36-week action handbook for theatre arts instruction

_____ **Introduction to Theatre Arts —**   **$29.95**
Teacher's Guide #BK-B265
by Suzi Zimmerman
Teacher's Guide to Introduction to Theatre Arts

_____ **Everything About Theatre #BK-B200**   **$19.95**
by Robert L. Lee
The guidebook of theatre fundamentals

_____ **Theatre Games for Young Performers**   **$17.95**
#BK-B188
by Maria C. Novelly
Improvisations and exercises for developing acting skills

_____ **Getting Your Kicks! (DVD with workbook)**   **$34.95**
#BK-DV06
A beginner's guide to choreography

These and other fine Meriwether Publishing books are available at your local bookstore or direct from the publisher. Prices subject to change without notice. Check our website or call for current prices.

Name: _____ e-mail: _____

Organization name: _____

Address: _____

City: _____ State: _____

Zip: _____ Phone: _____

❑ **Check enclosed**
❑ **Visa / MasterCard / Discover / Am. Express #** _____

Signature: _____   *Expiration date:* _____ / _____
                        (required for credit card orders)

Colorado residents: Please add 3% sales tax.
Shipping: Include $3.95 for the first book/DVD and 75¢ for each additional book/DVD ordered.

❑ *Please send me a copy of your complete catalog of books and plays.*